Concise guides to planning

Neighbourhood Planning in Practice

Neighbourhood Planning in Practice

Gavin Parker, Kat Salter and Matthew Wargent

LUND
HUMPHRIES

First published in 2019 by Lund Humphries

Lund Humphries
Office 3, Book House
261A City Road
London EC1V 1JX
UK
www.lundhumphries.com
Neighbourhood Planning in Practice
© Gavin Parker, Kat Salter and Matthew Wargent, 2019
All rights reserved

ISBN (hardback): 978-1-84822-283-0
ISBN (eBook PDF): 978-1-84822-284-7
ISBN (eBook ePub): 978-1-84822-311-0
ISBN (eBook ePub Mobi): 978-1-84822-312-7

Concise Guides to Planning (Print): ISSN 2516-8177
Concise Guides to Planning (Online): ISSN 2516-8185

A Cataloguing-in-Publication record for this book is
available from the British Library.

Designed by Stefi Orazi Studio
Cover illustration by Stefi Orazi
Set in Favorit

Image credits
p.61 (top) ECA Architecture | Planning | Community and
Boscombe and Pokesdown Neighbourhood Forum,
(bottom) ImaginePlaces Ltd working with Kentish Town
Neighbourhood Forum; p.62 Stowey Sutton
Neighbourhood Planning Group; p.78 ImaginePlaces Ltd
working with Elephant and Walworth Neighbourhood
Forum; p.79 Planning Aid England; p.80 Colyton
Neighbourhood Planning Group; p.82 Malborough
Neighbourhood Planning Group; p.95 Jake McNulty
and the Buckingham & Winslow Advertiser; p.128 Feria
Urbanism, Swale Borough Council and Faversham
Town Council.

Contents

Foreword

This inspiring book will be a boon for those wanting to find out more about how to become engaged with Neighbourhood Planning. It is written by a uniquely well-qualified team of experts who have been involved with local groups over many years. Targeted primarily at what they refer to as the 'citizen-planner' — those members of the community coming new to plan-making — the book reveals the opportunities and limits involved, by navigating through the process of creating a Neighbourhood Plan from start to finish. This introduction to Neighbourhood Planning will also be useful to professional planners wanting to know more about what is involved for them and also to students coming new to the subject. The text is lively and engaging, full of insights from practice, illustrated with a series of case studies and vignettes about how different groups have sought to make Neighbourhood Planning work for their localities. Read, enjoy, reflect and share.

Graham Haughton, Series Editor

Preface and Acknowledgements

This book focuses on the particular Neighbourhood Planning initiative that has been promoted in England since 2010. There are, of course, valuable experiences and lessons that have been drawn from similar forms of community engagement in planning in England and elsewhere, however the detailed review and advice here relates specifically to Neighbourhood Planning as constituted under the Localism Act (2011).

Neighbourhood Planning has been taken up by thousands of communities across England since it was first piloted. This new cohort of citizen-planners has found the experience empowering but also challenging. This is hardly surprising given that planning is a complex undertaking and the issues at hand are rarely resolved to the satisfaction of all parties. It is useful to note that the term 'citizen-planner' is one that we have adopted here to indicate those individuals who voluntarily engage deeply with formal planning and, most pertinently here, Neighbourhood Planning. The Neighbourhood Planning initiative is subject to a variety of constraints (not least the need to conform to existing planning policies) and often unpredictable variables (such as modifications made to regulations and changes in local circumstances). As a result navigating the Neighbourhood Planning 'space' can be difficult.

Most citizen-planners therefore embark on a journey of learning about their own community, the planning system, and any number of wider issues that impact on their own 'patch'. There is also a range of important relationships with local and national institutions that need to be nurtured. This book seeks to explain some of these issues and is particularly directed towards those considering or already undertaking Neighbourhood Planning. The coverage includes what to look out for, how to navigate the system, important relationships to develop and maintain, and the resources necessary to help produce a successful Neighbourhood Plan.

We have adopted a critical but supportive stance, explaining the types of issues and obstacles facing citizen-planners as shown through research and practice-based experience. We highlight ways to overcome difficulties and the benefits that can be secured. The authors have direct experience of supporting and researching Neighbourhood Planning communities, and this experience is drawn upon in the case studies that illustrate the issues being discussed. A set of resources and online links is also provided to guide the reader further in support of this book.

We wish to thank the team at Lund Humphries for their support during the writing of this book. The text has been inspired by the ethos of Planning Aid England who has been supporting communities in planning since the early 1970s. We would like to thank all citizen-planners who have lent their experiences, many of whom have kindly given their time to our research over the past eight years. Particular thanks go to the group of Neighbourhood Planners who gave us feedback on earlier drafts. It is ultimately your enthusiasm, determination and effort that makes citizen-planning possible, and we hope that this book will encourage and inspire others in return.

Chapter 1   **Introduction**

1.1 Aims of the book

The book is aimed at citizens and also professionals who want
to learn more about how Neighbourhood Planning operates
and how to navigate the process more effectively. Therefore
in addition to citizen-planners, this book should be useful for
professional planners in local authorities and those working
as consultants, who are often central to what are inevitably
'co-produced' Neighbourhood Plans. We use the term
co-production to refer to the way in which Neighbourhood
Plans are created, with partners working collaboratively to
successfully reach the completion of the Plan and hopefully to
see Plans being implemented. At its best, this process involves
sharing knowledge and capacity to produce Plans that have a
range of beneficial impacts on neighbourhoods.

Thus the book is written primarily for those interested in or
already involved in Neighbourhood Planning in England, as
formally enabled by the Localism Act (2011), the Neighbourhood
Planning Act (2017) and the associated Neighbourhood Planning
regulations. Hence when we refer to 'Neighbourhood Plans' the
focus is on Neighbourhood Development Plans (NDPs). If we
are making reference to something other than this policy vehicle
then it is made explicit in the text.

We have tried to write this book in such a way that it is
accessible; however, it is not jargon-free. There are a number of
technical terms used in planning that citizen-planners will need
to be aware of. Where technical language is unavoidable we
have sought to explain the terms involved in order to develop

awareness and ensure a working knowledge of the wider operating environment of Neighbourhood Planning. A Glossary is included at the back of the book to explain such jargon and frequently used terms. We have also provided some critical insight for those who wish to consider the research and theory that underpins the practice and issues tackled here (see Chapter 9, Section 2). We have also sought to break down many of the elements so that lists of key points are deployed to aid reference. On occasion we highlight in bold some of the critical statements that citizen-planners really need to absorb.

We feel it is necessary to point out that this book is not a technical guide about how to write a Neighbourhood Plan as there are other sources that provide such guidance (for example, Locality's widely read *Neighbourhood Planning Roadmap Guide*). Instead we provide the information to ensure that communities can navigate and embrace the ethos, spirit and possibilities of Neighbourhood Planning. This involves forming a realistic appraisal of the challenges involved. To achieve this balance we have developed **three core themes** that recur in the chapters that follow. These are:

- Neighbourhood Planning is *negotiative*: it should feature 'community-led negotiation' about the content and orientation of Neighbourhood Plans as well as ongoing relationships with other interested parties;
- Neighbourhood Planning requires *integration*: it must mediate between local and strategic concerns, local and expert knowledge, and sometimes the opposing forces of communities and the state – in other words, it is part of a wider system;
- Neighbourhood Planning is a *space of possibility*: it can be used to deliver community aspirations, added-value (for the planning system) and innovation, and can be the basis for further public participation, possibly providing a challenge to orthodox planning.

This book aims to explain Neighbourhood Planning in practice, drawing on experience of the planning system more widely and specifically on our experience of Neighbourhood Planning in England over the past eight years and the inherent challenges involved.

Thus while the book develops a detailed explanation of Neighbourhood Planning, we also feel that a broader understanding about how Neighbourhood Planning is shaped by higher-level plans and the involvement of other stakeholders is essential learning for citizen-planners and we have sought to assist the reader in developing such contextual awareness (Chapters 2 and 3). Recent experience indicates that citizen-planners who conceive of Neighbourhood Planning as an exclusively inward-looking exercise, instead of one that acts to bridge local and strategic concerns, will miss progressive opportunities and also often fail to secure the aims they seek. Therefore if communities avoid a more outward-looking sensibility, they are likely to run into problems and be left with a weaker Plan. As such, Neighbourhood Plans cannot be produced without developing an awareness of the roles and possibilities of partnering with others.

This echoes the aims of the book, which can be summarised as seeking to:

- Highlight the *key issues* involved in progressing a Neighbourhood Plan;
- Provide an overview of the *wider planning processes* that impact on Plan production;
- Explain the *roles, relations* and *skills* needed with others in Neighbourhood Planning;
- Establish ways of *overcoming the challenges* typically involved in Neighbourhood Planning;
- Provide *information, resources* and *examples* that will help set up readers on their journey to become 'critical' citizen-planners.

It is important to recognise the difficulties involved when participating in planning and this book is designed to enable a critical mindset that will help citizen-planners anticipate challenges and, if necessary, adjust their outlooks accordingly.

Therefore, we want to provide an appreciation of the likely challenges involved in order to provide citizen-planners with every chance of securing their aims and improving their local neighbourhoods. Experience has shown us that citizen-planners can often utilise the spaces of governance that are opened up by Neighbourhood Planning and use the new powers under the banner of localism, to secure at least some of their communities' desires.

It is important to stress that the book has been written during a period of uncertainty regarding the full impact of Brexit on some aspects of policy and regulatory requirements, particularly that which is conditional on EU regulations. Hence all such regulations we mention are inevitably subject to change. In reality this backdrop of conditionality or contingency is a fact of life in planning and there are plenty of other factors of change to be aware of, which are highlighted here.

Ultimately the process of completing a Neighbourhood Plan comes down to negotiating with other stakeholders such as local government, local landowners and housing developers. It is important to establish what the community wants and be mindful of other stakeholders' interests. *Neighbourhood Planning in Practice* sets out how citizen-planners can make the most of this opportunity to participate in local democracy, and we hope that a critically supportive stance will be helpful.

——

1.2 What is Neighbourhood Planning?

In 2010, the UK Government introduced a new statutory power for communities to produce a land-use planning document for their area, known as a Neighbourhood Plan. This was then enshrined in the Localism Act (2011) and later on modified by the Neighbourhood Planning Act (2017). Subject to meeting a series of criteria known as the Basic Conditions (see Glossary and Chapter 6), such Plans form part of the statutory development framework against which future planning decisions are assessed. The advent of these new citizen-led planning powers stemmed from a desire to utilise the knowledge, skills and time of local people rooted in their community. The rationale was succinctly expressed by the then Department of Communities and Local Government (DCLG) in 2012 as:

> ...in recent years, planning has tended to exclude, rather than to include, people and communities. In part, this has been a result of targets being imposed, and decisions taken, by bodies remote from them...and introducing Neighbourhood Planning addresses this.

The then newly formed Liberal Democrat–Conservative UK Coalition Government wanted Neighbourhood Planning to be central to a new planning system, one 'rooted in civic engagement and collaborative democracy', with a desire for people to become more involved in local decision-making and featuring greater citizen engagement in the planning system – in short to share control. These were rather grand (and not entirely new) aspirations and the rhetoric at the time was used deliberately to attract the attention of local residents and encourage them to embark on a Neighbourhood Plan.

Since those early days, all those involved in undertaking and researching Neighbourhood Planning have recognised the possibilities and effort involved as well as the inevitable limitations and constraints. Indeed questions still remain concerning the conditions placed on community inputs into the planning system and their ability to effect change.

Figure 1.1, overleaf, sets out in simple terms some of the possible benefits and likely drawbacks of Neighbourhood Planning that we will address in the book. Of course not every citizen-planner will have the same experience with their Plan, but after nearly a decade of practice, these issues are the ones that recur most often.

In short the aim of this book is to help secure more of the advantages whilst minimising the effects of the disadvantages. As we will explain in Chapters 2 and 3, there has been a feeling that the challenges involved in successful Neighbourhood Planning were downplayed, as was the traditionally adversarial nature of much planning activity and resultant development. Nonetheless thousands of local communities and citizen-planners

Some advantages and disadvantages
of Neighbourhood Planning

Typical NP Advantages	Typical NP Disadvantages
Greater *control* over new development (e.g. housing provision, size, design and location).	*Frustration*: there are limitations to Neighbourhood Plans and not everything the community wants will be delivered.
Opportunity to *increase well-being* for local community (e.g. green spaces, social assets).	*Time consuming*: Neighbourhood Plans take 2.5 years to complete, on average, but can take longer.
Opportunity to *secure community funding* – both small grants directly for the plan, and larger sums from CIL (see Glossary).	*Burdensome*: Plan production requires a large amount of work, especially for those leading the Plan on the Steering Group.
Opportunity to *attract businesses and employment* to the neighbourhood (where desired).	*Complicated*: Citizen-planners have to understand planning language and learn about a complicated planning system.
Greater *visibility and influence* with the Local Authority, and possibly with developers.	*Conflict*: planning is perhaps inherently conflictual; being able to make decisions comes with responsibility for those decisions, and these can sometimes create or deepen existing conflict.
Increased *community networking* and the opportunity to interact to exchange information and develop professional or social contacts.	
Increased likelihood of *delivering community projects*.	
Increased community *togetherness* and capacity.	

Figure 1.1

continue to take up the challenge and indeed have begun to reap benefits. It is this sense of enthusiasm that has driven the writing of this book, the main purpose of which is to help new citizen-planners navigate the process, achieve their aims and ultimately improve their built and natural environment. Our research has shown that Neighbourhood Planning involves significant learning for almost everyone involved and if this book can assist in this process then it will have done its job.

1.3 What does it mean to be a citizen-planner?

In the past there have been more limited opportunities for communities to participate in the planning system. For the first time, Neighbourhood Planning offers communities the right to produce a *statutory* planning policy document that reflects the views of the community and which should be used to determine planning applications.

In a sense anyone can become a citizen-planner, however to become effective and legitimately involved in Neighbourhood Development Planning, there are rules and processes to be followed. In Parished areas the Plan must be initiated by the Parish or Town Council (although anyone may be on the Steering Group – see Glossary). In non-Parished areas a Neighbourhood Forum must be set up; this requires 21 signatories drawn from a representative spectrum of local residents. At present the large majority of Neighbourhood Planning groups are in Parished areas, which are predominately rural areas. It can be more challenging to organise and agree the Forum composition and the neighbourhood boundary in non-Parished/urban areas (see Chapters 4 and 5), and time and patience may be needed to proceed through those steps.

Previous experience has shown that engagement with planning can be frustrating and attempts to address the so-called democratic deficit between community inputs and subsequent planning decisions have typically yielded unsatisfactory results. At the heart of this lies the question of *control* over the nature of citizen participation – who is involved, whose needs are catered for, and what priorities are recognised. Therefore, effective citizen-planners must ask themselves several important questions:

- What is it that we want as a community for our neighbourhood (and what tools are best suited to these aims)?
- What do we need to understand better (and what skills and resources are needed at each stage)?
- What knowledge, skills and resources are at our disposal (and where might additional knowledge, skills and resources be accessed if necessary)?
- How do we integrate the above into the making of the Plan?

These may seem like simple questions but it is important to reflect on them in order to identify gaps in understanding, skills or resources. For example, are there elements of the community whose views are not fully understood? What additional funding could the community obtain? Does the community have enough capacity (including time, skills and knowledge) to secure its aims? Are there useful contacts or networks that the community might draw on?

Thinking about these questions as early as possible is central to rooting the Neighbourhood Planning process in the wishes of the whole community and avoiding delays later in the process. Most communities, however small, will contain a variety of opinions and perspectives: it is therefore vital to reflect on the nature and variety of the community. This might include community leaders and existing groups (such as residents and housing associations or amenity societies) but also those whose voices are not often heard. It is vital to consider whether compromise is required, and which aims need to be adjusted or retained. This may also involve consideration of who we think about when reflecting on 'the community', and where certain relationships require proactive nurturing and methods of inclusion.

As we established in the previous section, Neighbourhood Planning involves a collection of interested parties and is therefore *negotiative*. What we mean by this is that

Neighbourhood Planning should feature 'community-led negotiation' about the content and orientation of the Plan whilst remaining aware of how this affects others. Neighbourhood Planning practice has revealed that in many ways community-led planning involves a series of community-led negotiations, and so the concept of negotiation is a central theme of this book. As strong as individual convictions may be, no one can succeed without the help and support of others, and so negotiation must be central to the identity of any citizen-planner.

In this spirit, it is important to think about the significance of the Neighbourhood Plan in symbolic terms, as well as a document made up of technical planning policies. Although the Neighbourhood Plan is a statutory document, it is worth remembering that it forms an important part of the negotiation of local decision-making and the way that it is written, organised and presented may prove a useful bargaining chip in future deliberations and decisions. In other words, citizen-planners should remember the emphasis on community-*led* planning and the need therefore for the community to *lead* negotiations and to be prepared to fight a particular corner, as well as being pragmatic about what can be achieved in local political settings. Indeed Neighbourhood Plans may be narrow or broad in scope to suit the specific conditions, resources and priorities of an area and so the challenges involved in preparing and implementing the Plan can vary.

This leads us to the second theme of this book: *integration*. To become a successful citizen-planner means not only reflecting on local concerns and knowledge, but also thinking about where these fit, or can be integrated into strategic concerns and with 'expert' forms of knowledge. More specifically, it also means considering how the Neighbourhood Plan will work in the wider planning system. This reflects how we see citizen-planning as part of a wider system where two worlds – local/strategic and community/state – are combined and more or less successfully integrated. In practice, to become a citizen-planner, it is necessary therefore to think about the concerns and perspectives of others – such as local government planners or local landowners – to understand the best way to secure community wishes.

Recognising the concepts of negotiation and integration is therefore central to becoming a citizen-planner. These two concepts are also required if communities are to utilise our third theme: seeing the overall process as a *space of possibility*, and attempting to innovate where appropriate. This is to say, that there is room to experiment in the Plan, to secure community aims that may not have been possible in the past, or to take responsibility for local development or local services that were previously controlled by private interests or local government. We return to this theme and give some concrete examples in Chapter 7. It is also worth remembering, as will be discussed further in Chapter 2, localism is largely about an ongoing negotiation between central government on one side and local government, communities and citizens on the other.

These three themes – *negotiation, integration* and *spaces of possibility* – may appear abstract, but as we aim to show they are central to becoming a citizen-planner. We hope that through the course of this book, readers can return to these themes and reflect on them as they are absorbed and understood alongside the details of Neighbourhood Planning. This requires us to be alert to how the ethos of Neighbourhood Planning, as originally conceived, was ostensibly about promoting community control. In practice Neighbourhood Planning has featured community-led, citizen-informed, co-produced effort. This presents an interesting dilemma as communities also need to liaise and learn about the formal planning and associated technical know-how that is deployed throughout the planning process. This may lead to trade-offs as individual groups are presented with choices on how to maintain the integrity of their efforts as communities while also ensuring their Plan reflects and aligns with the broader context.

This may set up a tension with a trend towards a 'professionalisation' of local knowledge and communities more generally. This has two aspects: first, in an operational sense, it is not necessary for citizen-planners to adopt wholesale the practices of professional planners and other partners (who will work to set parameters, timeframes and have established orthodoxies) and thoroughly learn all the technical elements involved in wider planning. Second, community interest, knowledge and experience does not need to be fully absorbed or subsumed into the black-box of 'professional' expertise.

It is therefore important for citizen-planners to remember that ultimately it is their Plan. While communities will necessarily need to draw on advice and expertise of others, it is important to try and retain community ownership as far as possible. The experience provides communities with the opportunity to develop skills and knowledge that will inform future participation within the planning system, feed into future decisions, and ultimately make it more likely that communities secure their aims.

As a Neighbourhood Plan progresses, citizen-planners may find their position shifting as different skills, knowledge and input are required at the different stages (e.g. at various points the citizen will be the client, at others a liaison officer, the author, and so on). There is a need therefore to be flexible without trampling on pre-existing agreed views of the community. Citizen-planners are at the middle of the network with various components required to assemble the Plan. The Steering Group – a term we use to denote the core group of community members who will orchestrate the Neighbourhood Plan – needs to be alert to these components and the different inputs required in order to successfully deliver the Plan.

We also feel it is crucial for citizen-planners to understand the contingent context in which Neighbourhood Plans are made. As we shall see it is likely that national and local planning policy will change during the course of Plan production, and so might the individual planning officers and politicians with whom communities must liaise. These obstacles are beyond communities' control, but it is nonetheless important to be aware of such possibilities in order to minimise disruption to the Plan in the longer term. It is therefore critical to understand from the outset what Neighbourhood Planning involves and its possibilities, limits, rules and challenges. Otherwise even the most well-meaning citizen-planner can easily lose the purpose of the Plan.

1.4 How to use this book

This book has been organised in such a way that it can be read chronologically or selectively dipped into in order to consider particular issues in the process. The intention is that advice is presented in a straightforward way but with an accompanying narrative that helps highlight where other Neighbourhood Planning communities have encountered problems and delays or have otherwise been less well prepared than they might have been. Examples from practice have been interspersed throughout the text to highlight key points, and we have provided a few key learning points and actions at the end of each chapter. The book is structured as follows:

- Chapter 1 – the introduction here serves to explain the approach taken, the structuring ideas, wider content and how to get the best from the book;
- Chapter 2 serves to outline the *basics of Neighbourhood Planning* including its background, the stages involved and the aims of both government and communities;
- Chapter 3 sets out an *overview of the English planning system* as it pertains and affects Neighbourhood Planning. This is necessary as a Neighbourhood Plan is part of a wider system and is therefore shaped by that system;
- Chapter 4 focuses on the *key relationships* with the various partner institutions that citizen-planners will encounter and work alongside in the development of their Neighbourhood Plan;
- Chapter 5 sets out *the stages* involved in Neighbourhood Planning in more detail;
- Chapter 6 establishes the *common hurdles and challenges* for communities involved in Neighbourhood Planning and advice on how to combat them;
- Chapter 7 explores some of the *ideas and opportunities* on offer to citizen-planners, including policy examples that could be applied to a neighbourhood plan;
- Chapter 8 concludes the book by *reflecting on the Neighbourhood Planning process* and reviewing the lessons presented by the text;

- Finally, Chapter 9 includes a useful list of *references, resources and support*.

Actions

In order to consolidate the coverage in this chapter and before proceeding with Neighbourhood Planning activity, be sure to look at the Glossary at the back of the book and to make a note of the key terms and other planning tools that seem relevant.

Ensure also that the key themes of *negotiation, integration* and *possibility* that we have introduced are kept in mind and carried through as the following chapters are absorbed. These, coupled with a recognition of the *phases* we identify (see also Chapter 4), should be borne in mind and allied to the appropriate mix of *resources* (split across the subcategories of money, time, partners, knowledge and influence) that are needed to navigate any given task or stage of Neighbourhood Planning. Our final tip is to take a look at Chapter 8 now (and to note Figure 8.1 on p.143), before proceeding through the book in a more orthodox way.

Chapter 2   **What is Neighbourhood Planning?**

▬

2.1 Introduction

This chapter explores Neighbourhood Planning in more depth, discussing its background and its emergence as part of the formal planning system. The other stakeholders involved in the production of a Neighbourhood Plan are also introduced before we reflect on what we have learnt in the past eight years of Neighbourhood Planning practice.

▬

2.2 Background to Neighbourhood Planning

Creating opportunities for communities to engage in planning in England has been an issue that successive governments have struggled with for decades. The role of the public in planning policy goes to the heart of questions of control, the public interest and ultimately who planning is 'for'. The widely supported desire to position communities more centrally in planning stems from disenchantment with planning outcomes throughout the post-Second World War period, but also from a lack of understanding about how the planning system works, and the rationale for decisions made by both local and national governments. These ongoing issues mean the perceived fairness of planning has long been questioned in many quarters.

Neighbourhood Planning has therefore emerged in an environment framed by persistent dissatisfaction with planning outcomes. While serial efforts to facilitate engagement over the decades have been made, they have been, on the whole, rather unsatisfactory in terms of generating innovation in planning outcomes, or ameliorating popular perceptions of planning as a *fait accompli*. Critical analyses from practitioners, academics and journalists have lamented the efforts of both central and local government to involve the public – while only periodically discussing how to better enable citizen participation. Ultimately these factors have added fuel to popular discontentment with the planning system.

This situation has presented successive governments with serious challenges when seeking to deliver much-needed housing and development while ensuring that local communities are effectively consulted and involved more fully during the planning process. As a result planning outcomes have appeared to lack nuance and, perhaps more importantly, legitimacy. It has long been hoped that a form of citizen-led planning could provide a space for community voices to be heard and thereby place community needs and aspirations closer to the heart of planning policy.

There have been some useful experiments with forms of citizen-led planning in England over recent years, such as parish planning and community-led planning, and these have acted to inform present attempts at neighbourhood planning (see Glossary). Neighbourhood Planning, as conceived in England, has been introduced under the aegis of the Localism Act (2011) and has a particular procedural frame – indeed, in order to facilitate the statutory status of Plans, there are a number of marked differences compared to previous forms of citizen-led planning. For example, Neighbourhood Plans have a more limited focus on land-use planning issues. They have a regulatory process that must be followed (including an independent examination and community referendum) and once 'made' the Plan forms part of the statutory planning framework against which planning applications will be assessed. One crucial consequence of this last characteristic is that Neighbourhood Plans must be in 'general conformity' with higher tier plans set by local and central government (such as Local Plans and the National Planning Policy Framework [NPPF]; see Chapter 3).

Localism in England
At the time of the 2010 UK General Election, the longstanding

issues of lack of engagement and public understanding of planning were unified with several other social concerns, such as the failures of 'big' government and state interference, and the lack of housing provision across the country. The newly elected UK Coalition Government therefore sought to simplify the planning system (notably through reducing planning guidance and removing Regional Spatial Strategies) but also to rescale it – pushing responsibility downwards to Local Authorities (LAs) (through Local Plans) and further still to neighbourhoods (through Neighbourhood Plans). The rhetoric at the time featured the idea of the 'Big Society', a rather amorphous policy agenda that consisted of decentralisation, the 'opening up' of public services, and increasing voluntary and social action, which was designed to redress the 'failures' of more interventionist governments that had gone before.

For the first time, the Localism Act (2011) placed statutory planning responsibilities at the hyper local scale with a community-led toolkit. This sought to make planning more innovative and accessible to different inputs through what was labelled 'Open Source Planning' (see Chapter 9, Section 1 and Section 3). This implied that a reformed planning system would encourage a wider range of inputs, including local knowledge and expertise from non-professionals. The concept was that Neighbourhood Plans would be rooted in popular decisions that could accommodate new development and maintain or reflect community support. It was this legislation that supported the introduction of a series of 'Community Rights' and associated tools, of which Neighbourhood Plans are one.

Previous experiments with community-led planning had been undertaken with some signs of success and so Neighbourhood Planning, as the latest iteration, went further than any other by granting community-produced Plans statutory status alongside higher tier planning policy. The array of tools on offer also includes Neighbourhood Development Orders that can be created by neighbourhoods to establish the principle of development on given sites. Similarly, the Community Right to Build gives communities the power to build new shops, housing or community facilities without going through the normal planning application process. Beyond these are rights (or policy tools) relating to community ownership of assets through Assets of Community Value and the ability to halt the sale of a building or land through the Community Right to Bid, which gives that community time to develop a bid to buy and run that asset. The Neighbourhood Plan has proved most popular given its comprehensive nature and, as explained in Chapter 1, it is the tool that forms the focus of this book. Further information on the other tools mentioned here are provided in the Glossary located towards the end of the book.

Generally speaking, the localist spirit that such tools represent requires decision-making to be made at the lowest appropriate level and therefore closer to those affected by the subsequent decisions. Recently this has been framed as redressing the balance of power between the state and citizens or communities. This has been heavily critiqued in some quarters, not least where particular forms of localism appear to make local people responsible for priorities that have been pre-set from above. Nonetheless the recent turn to localism since 1997 under New Labour and continued after May 2010 by the Conservatives (and Liberal Democrats in coalition) can be viewed as redressing, in part, the longstanding centralisation of political and administrative power across the UK throughout the twentieth century. For this reason, it can be useful to think of localism, not simply as a 'devolution' of power from central to local government or central government to communities and citizens, but also as an ongoing power struggle between the centre and the local. Done well, citizen participation in the name of localism can add legitimacy and transparency to decisions, and improve outcomes whilst inculcating a sense of being a public citizen: taking a share of responsibility for decisions and their outcomes. The opportunity for citizen-planners through Neighbourhood Planning, therefore, is to apply such new combinations of responsibility and empowerment locally to the best effect possible.

In this regard, Neighbourhood Planning has already provoked widespread discussion amongst communities, professional planners and academics. Many of the debates consider issues such as the value of the activity for both communities and the planning system (including how to keep up with political and policy change), questions of inclusivity and social justice, as well as practical issues such as the navigability of the planning system. We address many of these topic areas in the following chapters. Our overall approach is to explain the possibilities, potential pitfalls and lessons of Neighbourhood Planning specifically, however, through this approach common issues are raised that are of relevance to similar and parallel forms of community-led planning.

—

2.3 What is Neighbourhood Planning?

Neighbourhood Planning was initiated in response to a commitment to transfer power to local communities as part of a wider decentralisation agenda. The purpose of Neighbourhood Planning is understood as giving:

> communities direct power to develop a shared vision for their neighbourhood and shape the development and growth of their local area. They are able to choose where they want new homes, shops and offices to be built, have their say on what those new buildings should look like and what infrastructure should be provided, and grant planning permission for the new buildings they want to see go ahead. Neighbourhood Planning provides a powerful set of tools for local people to ensure that they get the right types of development for their community where the ambition of the neighbourhood is aligned with the strategic needs and priorities of the wider local area. (NPPG, Para 1; Reference ID: 41-001-20140306)

This is based on the premise that people know their area best and that if communities are empowered to shape their area this will lead to a more positive and less conflict-ridden approach to development. The desire to empower communities in this way sits alongside, and sometimes comes into conflict with, the broader desire for economic growth and increased housing development. As such, a range of incentives was simultaneously introduced to encourage communities to accept housing growth, including the New Homes Bonus and amendments to the Community Infrastructure Levy (CIL). The latter scheme includes an enhanced level of receipts (i.e. monies received to pay for infrastructure when new development proceeds) for communities who have developed a Neighbourhood Plan.

It is worth noting that at present not all Local Planning Authorities (LPAs) are progressing with CIL and it is recommended that Neighbourhood Planning groups appraise themselves of their LA's position and intentions regarding CIL and, where it is in place, consult the 'charging schedule' and accompanying policy regarding how receipts are to be spent. Moreover, it should be remembered that the rules surrounding CIL may well shift and in this respect it is probably ill-advised to undertake a Neighbourhood Plan solely due to the possibility of CIL monies (see Chapter 7). It is also important to bear in mind that community benefits may also be delivered through Section 106 agreements (see Glossary and NPPG) that are often negotiated between the LPA and a developer and attached to a planning permission to 'make acceptable development which would otherwise be unacceptable in planning terms'.

One of the attractions of Neighbourhood Planning is the opportunity for communities to set out their vision for their neighbourhood in a relatively self-contained way. However, it is important to recognise that the process does not exist in isolation – it forms part of a wider planning hierarchy and is framed by legislation that sets the parameters for its operation. As a result, higher tiers of planning policy act to frame and shape the Neighbourhood Plan (see Chapter 3). Central government sees Neighbourhood Planning as enabling sustainable development and as such Plans need to be positively prepared and should not promote less development than set out in the Local Plan or otherwise undermine its strategic priorities. Therefore, the presumption in favour of sustainable development is in-built within Neighbourhood Planning's procedures (see Chapter 3, Section 2).

There are a number of stages involved in the Neighbourhood Planning process – such as community consultation, evidence collection and the community referendum, all set out in detail in Chapter 5. In practice the process is more involved than progressing through a series of discrete, idealised stages and it is more time-consuming than other instances of engagement in planning where inputs may involve only one task or interaction, for example, writing a letter of objection or writing comments on a Local Plan draft. The later chapters of this book will address the key elements of this process, as well as those issues that are just as important but not well illuminated through a focus on the formal stages only.

2.4 Aims of Neighbourhood Planning

Central government has been at pains to stress that Neighbourhood Plans could be as broad or specific as each individual community wishes, but they should aim to add value to or address omissions in the relevant Local Plan. Therefore Neighbourhood Plans have to conform to the existing (and in practice, emerging) strategic policies but with scope to shape policies to suit local circumstances and engage with as many or as few issues as desired. A key limitation however is that whatever the scope decided upon by the community it has to relate directly to 'land-use planning'. This has proven problematic for many Steering Groups who have found that the wider community often wishes to tackle a wide range of issues, often well beyond land-use planning. A simple but highly useful question to consider when thinking about a potential Neighbourhood Planning issue is therefore: can this be determined through the operation of the planning system? That is, does it relate to a change of use, a possible condition on a planning application, or otherwise shape the design, location or type of development in the neighbourhood?

In terms of substantive outcomes, i.e. the kinds of development that can be directed through Neighbourhood Plans, there is little limit in theory (beyond larger infrastructure projects) as long as the policies and provisions found in the Plan do not contravene the strategic policies of the local plan, and that the likely development meet the tests for sustainable development set out nationally (see Chapter 3). In line with Neighbourhood Planning being a negotiative endeavour, establishing community projects and appropriate policies will typically require the Steering Group to liaise with other interested parties such as developers wishing to deliver housing projects, the LA looking to redevelop their assets or landowners contemplating how to best to utilise their land (as discussed in Chapter 4). These particular relationships may be both part of Neighbourhood Planning and separate from it. For example, Neighbourhood Planning cannot stipulate that Council land be turned into allotments, but policies for the protection of green spaces may be stipulated in the Plan whilst the Steering Group might also negotiate with the Council about the provision of allotments.

It is important to remember that many of the ideas the community may want to pursue can take months or years to come to fruition, often beyond the length of time it takes to complete a Plan. Overall this means that Neighbourhood Planning policy can cover any and all of the land uses (retail, offices, industrial, housing and so on – see Glossary term UCO) but that the financial resources to deliver the policy intent will almost always be derived from others. Making a Neighbourhood Development Order (NDO; see Glossary and p.133 in Chapter 7) could be a useful option, instead of or alongside the NDP, where a particular project and associated development emerges as important and where funds could conceivably be raised to implement it (examples could be a new community centre or a small development of affordable houses).

The relation between what might be called 'top-down' (i.e. strategic policy made by local and central government) and 'bottom-up' planning (i.e. citizen-planning) is an interesting one. The Neighbourhood Plan cannot overthrow strategic policy and the aim must be to apply it appropriately and positively plan for local needs derived from robust evidence. It is also worth noting that other development may still take place that is not explicitly recognised by a Neighbourhood Plan – but such activity will still need to conform to policy nationally, locally and at the neighbourhood scale (if relevant policies are included in the Neighbourhood Plan).

This leads us to the Basic Conditions, which are set out in Example 2.1 below (the formal 'framework' of the wider planning system is outlined in Chapter 3). These are seemingly broad and not onerous, but actually both are very important and also open to some interpretation – given the way that planning policy and guidance changes and the conditional need for some aspects of regulatory requirements such as Strategic Environmental Assessment (see Glossary), which may, given Brexit, soon change.

There have been a number of changes to Neighbourhood Planning since its inception in 2010 that reflect both legislative processes and how the Government has sought to 'speed up and simplify' the process due to experience of implementation. While the legal framework for Neighbourhood Planning is established in the Localism Act (2011), changes made to the regulations and, more recently, the Neighbourhood Planning Act (2017) reflect how the process has evolved over time. Key aspects of Neighbourhood Planning have also been clarified by the High Court as a result of developers challenging the content and premise of emerging Neighbourhood Plans. For example it has been established that a Neighbourhood Plan *can* be prepared and made in advance of a Local Plan. This increasingly judicialised environment has led to frustration from groups as the bar has been raised in terms of the level of evidence required to support the policies in Neighbourhood Plans. The 'light touch' regulatory approach to Neighbourhood Planning initially advocated by Government has seemingly been replaced by a more robust, technical approach. This is arguably necessary to ensure that a Plan stands up to the rigours of implementation.

Example 2.1   **Neighbourhood Development Plans —
the Basic Conditions**

The Basic Conditions for a Neighbourhood Plan to be considered adequate (as detailed in Schedule 10 of the Localism Act 2011) are:

- Having regard to national policies and advice contained in guidance issued by the Secretary of State, it is appropriate to make the Order;

- The making of the Order contributes to the achievement of sustainable development;
- The making of the Order is in general conformity with the strategic policies contained in the development plan for the area of the authority (or any part of that area); and
- The making of the Order does not breach, and is otherwise compatible with, European Union obligations.

(Note: the term 'Order' used above refers to the Neighbourhood Plan here)

Central government has responded to some of these 'teething problems' by not only introducing new legislation but also by funding Neighbourhood Planning and offering groups some grant aid, technical support and access to improved resources and guidance. These resources range from advice on the process, best practice, case studies to assist with peer-to-peer learning and more technical advice on, for example, how to carry out a Housing Needs Assessment (see Glossary). While these may be useful, the advice offered is 'general' and groups are advised to retain a discerning mindset about whether the advice is appropriate for their area (both in terms of geography and issues in the locality) and whether it reflects the current situation. It is especially important, for example, to ensure that resources are not out of date and whether fresh evidence may be required.

From the above description we can see that Neighbourhood Plans need to conform to, as well as supplement, the formal hierarchy of planning policy and plans. This can destabilise Neighbourhood Plans as change from above will impact on Plans created below (this can be a source of some frustration and needs to be considered throughout). Neighbourhood Planning therefore acts as a mechanism to elaborate what is intended nationally and locally – to interpret and develop policy so that it fits the neighbourhood situation. This may, in the case of housing development, mean thinking about questions of location, scale, timing, design and tenure of that housing. Other relevant items that need to be considered include a variety of area-based policies usually expressed through different planning designations. These carry either extra constraints on development or act to relax usually applied rules. These issues are important for citizen-planners because they alter the frame of operation for a Neighbourhood Plan, and we consider these types of issues in Chapters 3, 5 and 6.

—
2.5 Who is involved in the planning system?
Planning has historically been the preserve of professional planners working in the public sector, supplemented by inputs from a wide range of private-sector consultants. Other key interests are active through special interest organisations and include conservationists (e.g. Royal Society for the Protection of Birds, The Wildlife Trusts), environmentalists (through organisations such as Campaign to Protect Rural England, Friends of the Earth) and heritage activists (e.g. SAVE Britain's Heritage, The Society for the Protection of Ancient Buildings). Landowners and developers will typically promote their sites and seek to influence Plans to suit their interest. Members of the public have been offered limited opportunities to be involved, largely as consultees or as objectors, with individual schemes in the past. Hence why Neighbourhood Planning as the first statutory tool to be citizen-led has caused such excitement and drawn such attention.

As we have seen, there have been various changes to Neighbourhood Planning since its inception and these form part of broader reforms to the planning system. This change and the resultant impacts on citizen-planners is a cause for some concern as volunteers might reasonably expect that a task is set and that it can be mapped and completed following a set of rules and guaranteed parameters for 'success'. In planning this is rarely the case as the contributory issues that form the substance of planning activity shifts and plan-making takes just enough time to be caught up in a policy change, a ministerial decision or a legal judgement that appears to alter the parameters of robust and defensible policy. Such changes can also act to strengthen some ideas or aspects of a Plan.

One example is the way in which Objectively Assessed (Housing) Need (OAN; see Glossary) rules were reviewed in 2017. This has led to Local Authorities needing to revisit their existing housing figures and apply a standardised approach to assessing housing need. In some areas this has been leading to an increase and as a result could have implications for the housing levels expected in any given neighbourhood. Such alterations and new evidence is a feature of the planning environment and needs to be anticipated where possible, absorbed where necessary and added to a list of matters to address at a Plan refresh or review stage (see Chapters 5 and 6). In essence, such a complex undertaking can never be a matter of perfection. It is a matter of being flexible and adept at identifying what matters to the community – although it does bring into view how future approaches to Neighbourhood Planning may need to be more aware of the difficulties that such changes make for lower-level Plans and their durability. It also highlights how appropriate resources and support for Neighbourhood Planning are critical to its longevity.

Whilst Neighbourhood Planning is ostensibly community-led, in reality plans are co-produced by a range of groups and institutions. As will be discussed in more detail in Chapter 4, the relationships between these key stakeholders is a critical consideration for citizen-planners and a key set of variables in the speed and quality of the subsequent Neighbourhood Plan.

The key players involved in Neighbourhood Planning are:

- *Neighbourhood Planning groups* – the Qualifying Bodies and the communities they represent. We identify the members of such Qualifying Bodies and the active members of the community as citizen-planners who will craft the Neighbourhood Plan. The Neighbourhood Plan Steering Group is usually a smaller team appointed or assembled to take a lead on the Plan for the Qualifying Body;
- *Consultants* – often employed by communities to help manage the Neighbourhood Planning process and to input expertise at different stages of the process; also consultants operating as government-funded advisors (such as Locality);
- *Developers and landowners* – may have an interest in parcels of land within the neighbourhood area and will submit planning applications for development. Communities

need to engage openly and transparently to understand if the Plan proposals are deliverable and implementable. Developers may also try to circumvent the process and challenge Neighbourhood Plans through the High Courts as they seek to maximise their interests.

- *Local government* (i.e. the Local Authority and the Local Planning Authority) – the role of local government is multiple in terms of the impact on Neighbourhood Planning. This includes the production of the strategic policies of the Local Plan, fulfilling a series of legislative duties and 'duty to support' Neighbourhood Planning groups in their area;
- *Central government* – the responsible department for planning is the Ministry of Housing, Communities and Local Government (MHCLG; see Glossary) who will be instrumental in developing guidance, drafting new planning policy and preparing iterations of regulations guiding Neighbourhood Planning;
- *Independent examiners* – their role lies in determining whether the Neighbourhood Plan meets the Basic Conditions and legislative requirements at the examination stage.

The various roles and influence of these key partners are also explored in Chapters 4, 5 and 6.

—

2.6 Reflections

Given that thousands of communities in England have embarked on the process, Neighbourhood Planning to date can be said to have enjoyed some success. However the true test of success may be measured in how Plans add value to the community, pre-existing policy and the built and natural environment. It is vital therefore that Plans are robust enough to withstand the scrutiny of the development industry and are clear and implementable for the main user groups, i.e. local planning officers determining planning applications and the developers. Indeed a paper by Wargent and Parker (2018) argues that Neighbourhood Planning requires clearer and more ambitious criteria against which success may be measured (see Chapter 9,

Section 2). Our view is that a Plan that can lay claim to authority must be inclusive, it must be responsible and reflect the need both locally and more widely as well as adding value to existing planning policy. In short, the Plan should exhibit those qualities that make it equitable, defensible and valuable. We hope that the following chapters will help attain such measures of a successful Neighbourhood Plan.

Actions
In order to consolidate the coverage in this chapter, ensure understanding of:

- Neighbourhood Planning as a complex undertaking and that there are numerous partners with whom to develop a relationship (see also Chapter 4);
- The fact that planning and its context changes frequently and this needs to be understood and embraced;
- The overview of Neighbourhood Planning provided by support organisations, such as Locality. We recommend their *Roadmap* document and updates via their website;
- What is said about Neighbourhood Plans in the National Planning Practice Guidance (NPPG) (see Chapter 3);
- The MHCLG Neighbourhood Planning briefings e.g. *Notes on Neighbourhood Planning* produced intermittently;
- What it says about Neighbourhood Planning on the relevant Local Planning Authority website;
- How other Neighbourhood Planning groups in the area have operated, in order to learn from and share experiences;
- What funding and other support may be available for Neighbourhood Planning.

Chapter 3   Communities and the
                             Planning System

3.1 Introduction

It is important that would-be citizen-planners are aware of how
the system operates and Neighbourhood Planning's position
within it. A Neighbourhood Plan is only one part of what is usually
termed the 'plan-led' system of decision-making about land use.
This means that each layer of that hierarchy must be in general
conformity with the tier above, while also adding an increased
level of detail and focus to address aims and needs that are
evidenced more locally. Neighbourhood Plans therefore need
to be integrated into this wider system of policy and higher level
plans, and all Plans should be oriented towards delivering
sustainable development outcomes (see also Chapter 9,
Section 3).

   Many citizen-planners are motivated by a desire to assert
more control over decisions that affect their lives and the future
of their community, and not many citizens are inspired to learn
about the intricacies of the planning system without some kind
of incentive. Nonetheless when embarking on a Neighbourhood
Plan, it is necessary to understand the context within which that
Plan will sit.

3.2 What does planning seek to achieve?

The overall aim of the planning system is to ensure a balance
between enabling development to take place and conserving
and protecting the environment and local amenities. This is
encapsulated in the rather nebulous concept of 'sustainable
development', which is difficult to define and even harder to

deliver. Sustainable development can be broken down into three elements:

- *Futurity* – planning for future generations and ensuring that long-term considerations are addressed;
- *Environment* – planning in ways that protect and enhance the (natural and heritage) environment;
- *Equity* – planning fairly for all sections of the population, including appropriate and necessary physical development.

Beyond those three elements, adequate and inclusive participation should feature as a legitimising thread in the process of making policy that serves sustainable development. This highlights how planning is not only about individual land uses but is also concerned with how needs, issues and elements can be addressed through development decisions. Alongside this the quality of new development and its relation to the existing built and natural environment is part of an important 'place making' role for planning. This latter consideration speaks of the opportunity to shape places that both work better and are valued by the community.

It has also been a long-held contention that planning operates in the 'public interest', in that decisions are made for the wider collective good of society. This is obviously a hard concept to pin down and continues to be the subject of much contestation and debate. Operationalising the public interest is therefore fraught with difficulty, even if decisions are backed up by evidence. Ultimately some decisions are based on judgement – sometimes professional and sometimes political, or more often a mixture of the two. Nonetheless it remains an important justification of planning's purpose and ensuring the responsibilities stressed in Chapter 2 are a basis for serving the public interest.

3.3 The planning system in England

When first embarking on a Neighbourhood Plan, it is tempting for citizen-planners to focus on instrumental questions of 'what must be done' and to think more or less exclusively in terms of the stages of Neighbourhood Planning set down in the regulations (see Chapter 5). However Neighbourhood Planning is not only about slavishly following prescribed steps. There are a number of key areas of knowledge and understanding that active citizen-planners must develop in order to plan successfully, not least in gaining or refining a wider appreciation of how the planning system works and how to navigate it.

The current planning system was forged in the aftermath of the Second World War. The Government under Clement Attlee implemented a radical system for dealing with development and orchestrating land use across the UK. The Town and Country Planning Act of 1947 was the organising legislation. This Act vested development rights to the state so that planning permission would be required when proposals for development were made. Furthermore, the newly formed LPAs were to produce a land-use plan to guide those future decisions. These Local Plans set out planning policies and identified how land was to be used, and thereby determined to a large extent what would be built and where, what uses were deemed appropriate and which areas might require protection. There have been numerous changes to the planning system in the intervening years, but a similar approach is still used today. At its best this system provides some certainty about what can and cannot happen and why. It is about managing change sustainably.

Today, national planning policy acts to shape the broad policy parameters to which all other policy must have regard. This is established and explained in the National Planning Policy Framework (NPPF) – a document that directs LPAs about the way in which their Local Plan should be orientated and deals with a number of core themes. As we shall see, the NPPF's policies must be taken into account in the preparation of Local and Neighbourhood Plans, and are a 'material consideration' in planning decisions (see Glossary).

While there are a number of different aspects of the planning system to highlight, Figure 3.1, overleaf, provides an overview of the arrangement of law, policy and plans and illustrates the relationship between the tiers. At the time of writing there were three formal tiers of planning in England:

- *National* – principally the National Planning Policy Framework (NPPF) and the National Planning Practice Guidance (NPPG), as well as decisions and statements handed down by the Secretary of State;
- *Local* – through Local Plans prepared by district or unitary authorities (LPAs) forming the 'development plan', which can comprise numerous elements;
- *Neighbourhood* – principally through the (optional) Neighbourhood Development Plans that were introduced in 2010/11. These become part of the Local Plan once 'made' and are therefore illustrated on the same 'tier' as the Local Plan.

Certain aspects of English Planning Law and regulations are influenced and informed by European Law, notably the EU Directives on Environmental Impact Assessment and Strategic Environmental Assessment (although this situation may change post-Brexit).

The planning policy hierarchy and key relations

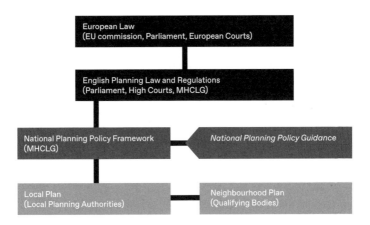

Figure 3.1

The simplified depiction in Figure 3.1 omits some parts that are unlikely to impact significantly on Neighbourhood Planning activity, but it is advisable that citizen-planners develop a basic awareness. For example a parallel approach to nationally significant infrastructure projects exists and the role that the Local Highways Authority plays in developing transport plans (see also Chapter 9, Section 3).

The citizen-planner must ensure that their Plan sits comfortably with the national policy framework and the relevant Local Plan, since in essence, the NPPF and the Local Plan act to 'frame' the Neighbourhood Plan. It may be useful to conceive of these tiers as 'nested' parameters that become more detailed as we pass down the hierarchy: overall a wide range of topic areas are covered in increasing levels of detail. The national level sets out the general principles and aims that plans and policies downscale should pursue. The Local Plan is the first level of planning that is explicitly spatial and deals with specific places. The Local Plan also applies the general policy direction to suit localised circumstances. Neighbourhood Plans, where they are pursued, should seek to complement and add further detail to the Local Plan. The following section explains this in more detail.

___

3.4 The planning framework

The planning system is 'plan-led', also each LPA is required to assemble a Local Plan that sets out how planning will be organised within their jurisdiction over a set period. These must conform with central government's planning policies as set out in the NPPF. The power to decide what Local Plans should consist of is held by local politicians (councillors or elected members within the council), although a significant amount of this work is now delegated to local planning officers. As we have seen, citizen involvement in this process has a significant, although often unsatisfactory, history in the form of consultations, written submissions, attendance at public meetings and engaging in civil disobedience.

The following sub-sections explain the levels of the planning system in more detail, starting with national policy.

National Planning Policy Framework (NPPF)

The NPPF sets out the Government's planning policies and how they are expected to apply. At the heart of the NPPF is the presumption in favour of sustainable development. This is crucial as it shows, explicitly, that the purpose of the planning system is to help achieve sustainable development. The policies in the NPPF, taken as a whole, constitute the Government's view of what sustainable development in England means in practice for the planning system. We advise that any citizen-planners familiarise themselves with this.

Example 3.1   **National Planning Policy Framework (NPPF) 2018**

The NPPF was first published in 2012 and replaced an extensive suite of policy documents. The 2018 framework incorporates changes to the Planning System made since 2012.

The NPPF provides a framework within which development plans can be prepared and for decision-making. It reasserts the *presumption in favour of sustainable development* and the importance of a plan-led system. The NPPF covers a wide range of topics including housing, economic development, transport, the natural and built environment and so on, with each chapter indicating a key area of concern for the Planning System.

The NPPF acts as a guide to begin to shape both local plans and Neighbourhood Plans. It also helps delineate the *limits* of land-use planning. It is imperative for Neighbourhood Planners to read the NPPF.

The first NPPF was finalised and came into operation in 2012. In 2018 a review was completed and includes further tweaks to the place of Neighbourhood Planning in the system, arguably to try and strike a balance between the delivery of housing in particular and to ensure that producing a Neighbourhood Plan remains worthwhile. What we can say is that the relationship between the Steering Group and the LPA and the Local Plan policies and evidence base is critical.

Despite any revisions, the NPPF acts to provide a framework within which local people and Local Planning Authorities can produce their own distinctive Local and Neighbourhood Plans, which reflect the needs and priorities of their communities.

In addition to the NPPF there are other national planning policies on Waste, Travellers, Planning for Schools Development, Section 106 Planning Obligations on Small-scale Sites, Sustainable Drainage Systems and Parking. Government Policy may also be altered by a Written Ministerial Statement (see Glossary).

National Planning Policy Guidance (NPPG)

The NPPF is supplemented by the National Planning Policy Guidance (NPPG). Since 2014 this has been published on an online portal and is regularly updated. This enables anyone to search for the policy and guidance applicable to any given planning topic. The NPPG supports the policies in the NPPF and provides further context. It acts to inform individual decisions and applicants when putting together their development applications. Those preparing Plans (both Local and Neighbourhood) must also have regard to the advice contained in the NPPG. The guidance is also a material consideration when taking decisions on planning applications (see Glossary). This means that if a local policy is deemed out of date, Local Authorities may be directed by the national guidance requirements. Updates and alterations are regularly made to this guidance and it will be wise to bookmark it to ensure that the emerging Neighbourhood Plan is shaped with regard to the relevant parts of it. What is relevant or germane to the plan will depend on what the Plan is hoping to achieve, and what policies and coverage it embraces.

Local Plans

Each LPA is required to assemble a Local Plan, which seeks to shape future development and address the needs and opportunities of the district or unitary area. The Local Plan sets the framework for how local decisions will be taken and the overall vision and strategic objectives on how the area should develop. Crucially, Local Plans set out how much development is needed over the plan period – typically 15 years – where, when and by what means it will be delivered. The Local Plan should allocate strategic sites that are considered central to the achievement of the strategy and this includes housing and employment allocations.

Local Plans are arguably the lynchpin of planning in England as they are the first consideration in deciding development proposals. The law makes it clear that decisions should be made in accordance with the policies and proposals within the Local Plan unless other strong planning reasons or material considerations indicate otherwise, and the policies must conform with central government's planning policies as set out in the NPPF. As we have seen, the ultimate power to decide the content of Local Plans falls to local politicians, but there is a prescribed process that must be followed, including consultation stages where members of the community and other interested parties will be formally invited to comment on the emerging Plan (see the NPPG on this). This provides an opportunity to submit any comments, concerns or suggestions on the emerging strategy and propose any changes to be made.

The Local Plan may comprise a series of documents, including a Core Strategy or Local Plan 'Part 1', which outlines the overarching strategic priorities and development framework. This may be supplemented by a Development Plan Document (DPD) that contains the detailed policies and site allocations. Other documents including Supplementary Planning Documents (SPDs) may be pertinent, for example, a Design Guide that many LPAs adopt. A policies map (sometimes referred to as a 'proposals map') will also be published that will show where development *could* take place, including the strategic housing and employment allocations. It should also identify areas of protection such as nationally protected landscapes, areas of importance for nature conservation and Green Belt.

Details of the current Policy Framework can usually be found on the LPA's website and should include the status of the Local Plan and whether an emerging Local Plan is being prepared. The idea is that the Local Plan embraces a number of policy themes and provides detail about how development in the locality meets needs and conditions. Local Plans must be based on a solid evidence base and pass an independent examination orchestrated by the Planning Inspectorate (PINS) appointed on behalf of the Secretary of State.

Neighbourhood Plans

Neighbourhood Plans are similar to Local Plans in several respects. They must be in conformity with higher tier policies and must be rooted in defensible evidence. Formally speaking, completed Neighbourhood Plans are 'adopted' as part of the local planning framework. It will be useful for all Neighbourhood Plan Steering Groups to become familiar with their own area's Local Plan and discuss its content and rationale with the local planning policy team.

Central government has been at pains to say that Neighbourhood Plans should not be 'mini-Local Plans'. This is because Neighbourhood Plans have to be in general conformity with the strategic policies in the adopted Local Plan; these policies should therefore be identified at an early stage in order to ensure the Neighbourhood Plan not only meets the required Basic Conditions but also to prevent existing policies being repeated. Indeed would-be citizen-planners may find that their Local Plan contains policies in sufficient detail that the goals of the community are already being met, and a Neighbourhood Plan may be redundant – although it should be remembered that there are many benefits to a Neighbourhood Plan (see Chapter 7). What Local Plans may not cover is a degree of detail or specificity about what happens in a particular neighbourhood.

In many areas Neighbourhood Plans are being prepared in advance of a Local Plan. The NPPG advises that, although a draft Neighbourhood Plan is not tested against the policies in an emerging Local Plan, the reasoning and evidence base is likely to be relevant to the consideration of whether the Basic Conditions are met. Local Planning Authorities should publish their evidence base online and take a proactive and positive approach and work collaboratively with those preparing Neighbourhood Plans in order to ensure they have the greatest chance of success at examination – this includes, in particular, sharing evidence and seeking to resolve any issues where there is disagreement (NPPG, para 9; Reference ID: 41-009-20160211).

There have been numerous issues where Neighbourhood Plans have been produced in advance of a Local Plan (or where the Local Plan is for some reason absent). This issue may diminish over time as Local Plans are updated, but a good understanding between the LPA and the Steering Group is needed and the Neighbourhood Plan will still need to accord with the NPPF. In areas without an up-to-date Local Plan in place the Neighbourhood Plan may come under increased scrutiny from developers as they will regard the Neighbourhood Plan as an important part of the Local Plan for that particular part of the district. This may mean that they also seek to challenge it (see Chapters 6 and 7).

3.5 Constraints and alternatives

It is important to remember that Neighbourhood Planning can be a useful tool to deliver neighbourhood objectives but it is not the only planning tool, nor the only method of democratic participation. There are a range of both statutory and non-statutory options available and the choice of which to progress can be a challenge in its own right. There are many things to consider when making this decision, including the issues you wish to address, the resources and time available and the status and strategy found in the Local Plan. A further consideration is the likelihood of policy aims being implementable through a Neighbourhood Plan. Examples of alternative planning tools are detailed in the Glossary (and see Chapter 9, Section 4). Furthermore, as we discuss in Chapter 7, some groups may decide to use more than one tool in combination to more comprehensively address issues affecting the community.

3.6 Reflections

Planning is a contested arena and tools and policies that service the system are routinely challenged. Often the criticisms come from those seeking to gain advantage or who have a limited view of the difficult or complex set of considerations that are being addressed through planning. There are numerous factors that can impact on a Neighbourhood Plan that each group will need to appreciate – some local areas may not have an up-to-date Local Plan, for example, or some aspect of national policy may change during the production of a Neighbourhood Plan. The chapter has explained the importance of a working familiarity with the wider planning system and indicated key sources of policy that will inevitably shape a Neighbourhood Plan. Indeed, the creation of Neighbourhood Plans and related tools were seen as mechanisms to engender greater awareness of planning and to develop a greater sense of responsibility for the future development of local environments.

The wider resources we provide at the end of the book should help further develop the necessary prior learning about planning and Neighbourhood Planning. This study will help ensure that the overall process 'fits' the requirements of the policy hierarchy – as well as identifying how to ensure the communities' views are heard.

Actions

In order to consolidate the coverage in this chapter, ensure liaison with or working knowledge of:

- The National Planning Policy Framework (NPPF) – to understand the approach generally and specifically policy in relation to Neighbourhood Plans;
- The Local Plan that serves the district or unitary area;
- The Planning Policy team at the relevant Local Authority;
- A nearby Neighbourhood Planning group (preferably within the same Local Authority area) who have made at least some substantive progress with their plan.

Chapter 4   **Relationships in Neighbourhood Planning**

4.1 Introduction

This chapter explains how citizen-planners can navigate the Neighbourhood Planning process effectively, managing key relationships and integrating their local experience and knowledge into the planning system. Building, nurturing and maintaining relationships is just as important as understanding Neighbourhood Planning's formal regulations or developing technical planning knowledge, as without the support and collaboration of other stakeholders and partners, Neighbourhood Planning can be a frustrating, if not impossible, task. This may sound daunting – and the relationships described in this chapter can also be fruitful and even enjoyable – but it would be remiss not to stress the importance of these relationships, and impress the importance of prioritising them from the very start of the Neighbourhood Planning process.

4.2 Managing relationships, negotiation and conflict

Any process involving multiple groups of people requires good communication, reciprocal understanding and co-operation, and Neighbourhood Planning is no different. What distinguishes Neighbourhood Planning from similar activities, however, are the technical, procedural and legal requirements of the process – despite the fact that the majority of the workload is shouldered by volunteers who may or may not possess experience of technical planning matters. This will strike a chord with many of those who have some experience of the planning system, in particular the sensitivities that arise around planning processes and outcomes, as well as the 'layers' of planning, as discussed in the preceding chapter, which can both constrain and enable planning at the neighbourhood scale.

In short, the complexity of Neighbourhood Planning lies not only in the substantive issues and the procedural requirements but also in the people involved and the often contentious politics of space and place. Much of the process is defined by the interaction between 'expert' (or 'professional') knowledge and the experience of community members (often referred to as local or 'lay' knowledge). Successful Neighbourhood Planning requires a brokerage system between strategic, local, technical and practical knowledge – particularly at the point between the community and Local Authority. Whilst there are other relationships that also require attention, the evidence shows it is this central dynamic around which successful Neighbourhood Planning pivots.

From the citizen-planner's perspective, successfully navigating this dynamic starts with the Steering Group itself. The group needs to be resilient and, as far as possible, maintain an optimistic view of planning and local issues, in order to 'plan positively' throughout the process. This entails avoiding revisiting old disputes or other outstanding issues that may have affected local attitudes in the past, being patient but also being clear about what the community needs and understanding where there are gaps and opportunities. Citizen-planners therefore need to be diplomatic and maintain good interpersonal relations with the LPA and the wider community in particular.

Figure 4.1, overleaf, shows the types of skills and inputs needed during the four overarching Neighbourhood Planning 'phases' (*preparation, drafting, finalisation* and *implementation* – see Chapter 5). Within each of these phases are the regulatory steps or stages of Neighbourhood Planning that are outlined and discussed in the next chapter. Relationship management is at the very centre of this diagram and this is stressed in order to underline how co-operation with others is central to the process and at the heart of all four phases – and ultimately therefore critical throughout the Plan-making project. The positive approach we recommend here can sustain a supportive operating environment in which it is necessary (or at the very least desirable) to progress a Neighbourhood Plan collaboratively.

It is useful to remember that not all of those with a role in the Neighbourhood Planning process will necessarily view the process as important or even worthwhile. In some cases reticent parties may be persuaded of Neighbourhood Planning's merits but others may be more steadfast in their opposition (see the discussion of challenges in Chapter 6). Nonetheless much of the research considering forms of community engagement stresses the benefits of learning by doing and the ways in which people develop new or strengthened networks both within their community and beyond. Developing a Neighbourhood Plan often requires deliberate forms of enrolment and recruitment activity in order to gain support and commitment. A Memorandum of Understanding or 'service level agreement' between the Neighbourhood Planning group and the LA is an example of such enrolment (see Example 4.1 and Glossary). This acts to structure the relationship; indeed the Local Planning Authority's Statement of Community Involvement has to specify more clearly the support offered (from summer 2018) and this aids the creation of such a 'contract'.

Example 4.1 **Memorandum of Understanding**

There are numerous examples of Memorandum of Understanding between Neighbourhood Planning Groups and the Local Authority including those produced by East Riding of Yorkshire Council and South Somerset. Care should be taken to ensure that the Memorandum of Understanding reflects your circumstances and need through the various stages of Neighbourhood Planning, including post-adoption i.e. to allow for arrangements when a Plan needs to be amended or refreshed.

Locality has published a useful guide: '*Developing a Memorandum of Understanding: a toolkit for Neighbourhood Planners.*' See: https://mycommunity.org.uk/wp-content/uploads/NP_Memorandum-of-Understanding.pdf

Negotiation

As we discussed at the start of the book it is useful to think of Neighbourhood Planning as a series of negotiations. Some points of negotiation are necessitated by regulatory process and others are more *ad hoc* and arise, for example, where the Steering Group wishes to secure buy-in from another party or ensure the quality and robustness of the Plan. This means that progression needs a number of soft skills and techniques that can be used to negotiate the community's position. This requires being alive to instances where the Steering Group might adopt the role of mediators working to reconcile or at least inform other interested parties about the Plan. Being aware of the pinch-points and critical relations (such as a lack of LPA support, a poorly briefed consultant, or the neglect of a section of the community) and how to manage these through a diplomatic and pragmatic approach to the process is highly advisable.

We have broken our discussion into two parts here, discussing internal and external relations in turn. Citizen-planners are at the very heart of the process working directly with other partners, and it is vital to be able to liaise effectively and adopt mediatory behaviours throughout the process. Such behaviours are typically grouped under three headings: listening, questioning and non-verbal communication (see Figure 4.1). These simple techniques if applied well can ease relations and bring out the best in partners in order to shape and hone the Plan. It may be that you have some adept communicators who are or could be involved in the Steering Group to assist in this aspect of Neighbourhood Planning.

Increasingly local planning decisions require numerous parties to co-operate. Typically participants can be categorised into one of the following three groups:

- Public sector (local and national politicians and civil servants, including local planners);
- Private sector (commonly property developers, landowners, planning consultants);
- Civil society (sometimes referred to as the Third Sector), this broad group includes individual citizens and communities, charities, social enterprises, residents' groups, housing associations and so on).

Supportive behaviours for Neighbourhood Planning

Listening (use the 'LISTEN' mnemonic)	Questioning style	Non-verbal communication tips
Look at the person.	Probe with 'Who, What, Why, Where, When, How' questions.	Use active listening – prompt and check.
Inquire with questions.	Use open/closed questions where appropriate to ensure clarity is given and received.	Match verbal signals – enable the other person to feel comfortable.
Stay on target – keep to an organised list of topics.	Use directive questions involving explanation.	Use open body posture – this stance brings out a more open position from the other person.
Test understanding – ensure that clarity has been achieved.	Ascertain who holds knowledge that is needed.	'Mirror' others, verbal and non-verbal, to confirm and assure.
Evaluate process – think about what is needed to help progress.	Ensure that answers received are understandable/ usable.	Use accessible and 'open' materials and outputs (such as website, flyers, updates) that encourage inputs and support.
Neutralise feelings – do not react if the information or response is not what is wanted.	Use non-emotive and neutral language and tone to clarify any implications and identify next steps.	Do not show disappointment but remain calm and open.

Figure 4.1

These categories are quite rudimentary and may of course overlap in some instances but it is worth being aware of the motivations, obligations and dispositions that representatives of each group are likely to possess. Also bear in mind that Local Authority planners – specifically the development management officers – will become key users of the Plan, and to aid implementation clarity and specificity are needed. Managing these relationships can be difficult for communities who are dealing with professional organisations whilst they themselves are participating voluntarily; difficulties can include interpreting specialist and technical language and being expected to work during business hours (see the discussion of 'professionalisation' in Chapter 1). Yet with preparation and clear communication, relationships with other stakeholders in planning can create mutuality and respect that make the Neighbourhood Planning process far less daunting, a little more enjoyable and ultimately more successful.

Resolving conflict

Probity and transparency is important in all planning activity and none more so than in Neighbourhood Planning when friends, neighbours and colleagues are affected and involved. Those engaging with the Neighbourhood Planning process will need to ensure that any potential conflicts of interest are declared and that the team leading the process keep a register of interests – this is important to ensure that probity is actually, and seen to be, maintained. Groups may wish to consider including a 'declarations of interest' register as part of the terms of reference for the Steering Group and expressed in the constitution for a Neighbourhood Forum (see Chapter 7 and Glossary). Potential conflicts include land ownership, share ownership (significant shares held in a company known to have a development interest in the area) and employment status. There are some, albeit few, examples in Neighbourhood Planning practice already where significant fallout and delay has been a product of this type of issue. Appropriate arrangements may have to be put in place, for example, this may mean in certain situations some members abstaining from voting. There are a number of examples available online of a declarations of interest register that can be used as a template.

4.3 Relationships within the community

It is crucial early on to understand the constituency – in other words to ask for whom are citizen-planners planning? This question has two central facets, firstly what is the geographical extent of the area? This may involve some discussion about how to delineate the neighbourhood to be covered by the Plan, especially in non-Parished areas. Secondly who is 'the community'? Although citizen-planners are not elected representatives like MPs or local councillors, it is still necessary to think actively about what is meant by 'community' beyond the simple geographic area (see Chapter 5) and who this should encapsulate.

The term 'community' may bring to mind a homogeneous or like-minded group of people, however even the smallest communities will be sites of disparate views and interests in planning outcomes. It is therefore vital to engage beyond the Steering Group and reach as many people as possible. This includes not only a breadth of residents but also businesses and those employed within the area. If carried through well this will ensure that the Plan represents, as far as possible, the widest range of views. It will also help to build up support for the Plan and make a successful vote at referendum more likely.

Maintaining relations within the community is critical given that the Steering Group will only ever comprise a small number of people and the Parish or Town Council or wider Neighbourhood Forum cannot be said to adequately represent the population sufficiently to reflect the views and attitudes or minimise possible disagreement or conflict in the neighbourhood. Much has been written about collaboration and participatory tools and techniques in participation (see Figure 4.2, overleaf). Creative use of such tools can enrich the process and generate better quality of data, information exchange and moreover ease possible tensions. Indeed inclusion is an important byword in planning at all levels and is recognised in national policy (notably the NPPF).

The transparency of participation is also important to maintain trust. It is important to remember that the process overall will be scrutinised on these grounds by the independent examiner and the Local Planning Authority. There is a need to ensure that all views have been considered and this forms part of the Basic Conditions test that will be applied at independent examination.

Participatory tools for Neighbourhood Planning

Participatory tool	Explanation	Relations focus (i.e. to help between group 'X' and 'Y')
Talking wall	Download ideas and issues in one place – often using stick-it notes. These can then be themed and organised. Such themes could then inform or shape further discussion.	A useful tool to ensure that the wider neighbourhood can see what others are saying about the area.
Charrette	Often used to think about design – it is a short, collaborative meeting during which attendees collaborate and share ideas in order to draft a solution.	To focus on key issues and ensure that those with different views are able to discuss solutions. Can aid the Steering Group to understand thinking behind issues and solutions.
Neighbourhood meeting	Open meeting to update and gain broad feedback. May have limited value beyond information sharing (which has its own value).	Another means to bring together the wider 'constituency' and make the Steering Group visible and accountable.
Action learning event	Where those present can work through issues and share ideas. The process involves taking action and reflecting upon results.	It can help to improve the problem-solving process and enable complex issues to be handled and resolved more effectively.

Community mapping	Where participants build up a map of what the neighbourhood is like and how it could be changed.	Planning for real is a form of this but models can be used or built to focus attention.
Focus groups	Where a small number of participants come together and engage in a deeper guided discussion.	To draw on respondents' attitudes, feelings, beliefs and reactions.
Questionnaires	A series of questions are asked in order to gain information from individual respondents.	To understand the spectrum of views and opinions held by those completing the questionnaire.

Figure 4.2

Figure 4.2 shows a number of tools that citizen-planners can employ. This list is not exhaustive and the resources section at the end of book points to further examples. It is important to remember that there is no 'one-size-fits-all' approach to this aspect of participation – it is more about tailoring the right tools to the community and ensuring the process is transparent and justifiable. Neighbourhood Planning is, in essence, a form of community appraisal that leads to a co-produced Plan 'led' by the community. The importance of such tools lies in their ability to strengthen the relationships that are central to the Neighbourhood Planning process, as well as to elicit important information and evidence with which to shape the Plan itself.

On a practical footing, there are three key points to consider:

- *Transparency* – the wider community needs to be able to follow progress of the Plan as it evolves (not just consultation and engagement stage points). This will mean keeping lines of communication open, such as updating social media and a web presence, conducting well-advertised, open meetings, publishing records of meetings including when decisions are made and why;

- *Flexibility* – consultation and engagement with the wider community can come in many forms and it is important to tailor the approach to the needs and characteristics of the community. Transparency should not come at the expense of a more inclusive approach. As also discussed in Chapter 5, there is a range of methods that can be adopted to ensure engagement and involvement from a cross-section of the population and not just the 'usual suspects';
- *Justification* – with transparency and flexibility in mind, the approach to consultation that is adopted must be justifiable in both a formal sense (i.e. to the external examiner) and an informal sense (i.e. to the wider community who must ultimately support and vote for the Plan).

Further materials and techniques are indicated in Chapter 9, Section 5.

Working relationships within the Steering Group
Notionally Neighbourhood Plans can be categorised by their location in Parished and non-Parished areas. In the former, only the Parish or Town Council (or group of Councils) have the power to develop a Neighbourhood Plan and to undertake the statutory stages (although in practice the task of Plan preparation is often devolved to a Steering Group – see below). In the latter instance, a group of 21 individuals who live in the neighbourhood area, work there and/or are elected members for a Local Authority that includes all or part of the neighbourhood area can come together to establish a Neighbourhood Forum (if the proposal meets the regulatory requirements).

In both Parished and non-Parished areas it is common practice for a Steering Group to be established and to lead the process. Such groups can be formed of Town and Parish Councillors (where this tier of government exists) as well as representatives of local community groups, residents and business leaders. In Parished areas, in order to meet the legislative requirements concerning Town and Parish Councils, the relationship between any group and the formal functions of the Town or Parish Council should be transparent to the wider public.

→
Canvassing
views of the
community,
Boscombe and
Pokesdown
Neighbourhood
Plan, Dorset.

→
Street
engagement:
'If I were Mayor
of Kentish Town
I would…'.

In all instances, it is important to consider what skills the Steering Group possess and the demographic profile of members. As far as possible the Steering Group should reflect a range of interests and perspectives and this may require actively enrolling and encouraging others to become involved. When this is done with sensitivity, the formation of a Steering Group should enable a broader range of views to be captured and for the workload to be shared. Many neighbourhoods have established further subdivisions to create working groups, typically around particular issues such as housing, heritage or green spaces. Again it is important that open and transparent processes are put in place to explain how these structures will operate, how decisions will be made and who is involved. Most Steering Groups also appoint a chair who leads the process in some capacity. Many groups install the chair into a *primus inter pares* position (i.e. a 'first among equals' role) that enables them to lead the process and keep the Plan on track without them having to assume responsibility for the whole Plan.

← Neighbourhood Plan Steering Committee Structure, Stowey Sutton Neighbourhood Plan, Somerset.

For most groups, terms of reference can prove to be an appropriate tool to structure and record the decision-making process (particularly in multi-Parished Neighbourhood Planning areas). The terms of reference can include information on: roles and responsibilities, membership, decision-making, meetings, working groups, finance, monitoring and implementation of the Plan and, as discussed previously, conflicts of interest. A project plan for the process is also a useful step for anticipating what needs to be done and who will lead on implementing it (see Chapter 6, Section 3.

—

Example 4.2   **Terms of Reference for Neighbourhood Planning groups**

There are numerous examples of Terms of Reference for Neighbourhood Plans available online, including 'Sample Terms of Reference' produced by Rutland District Council, Herefordshire County Council and Cornwall County Council
    Planning Aid England has published a case study of Roseland, Cornwall, in which they explain how they organised and ran their Steering Group. See: www.ourneighbourhood planning org.uk/case-studies/view/303

—

4.4 Relationships outside the community

Neighbourhood Planning cannot be successful without the support and inputs of others. This relates directly to co-production and negotiation in planning. Co-production is a process characterised by the sharing and integration of knowledge, capacity and priorities. A close relationship between those traditionally affected by planning and those traditionally involved in implementing policy can act to provide better outcomes for all parties if adopted. Such relations can become challenging unless mediated deftly. This is because existing working practices or cultures within government and any consultants that have been brought in to assist the community will differ. Other parties and LPAs are necessarily altered, or accommodated by greater involvement from communities. This process of integration rarely occurs without debate, and often tension, due to the dilution of power and control that is usually involved.

The principal external partners for Steering Groups are the LPA partners, which may include landowners and developers (who may or may not fall neatly into an internal/external divide), as well as a multitude of other stakeholders such as heritage, biodiversity or community organisations and in non-Unitary areas the County Council (as Highways and Minerals and Waste Planning Authority). As with previous forms of community-led planning the importance of developing a positive and respectful working relationship with key partners cannot be underestimated. Time and effort should be put into building up connections and trust between groups (face-to-face interaction always helps here), and a willingness to debate key priorities, both shared and disputed.

There may be points within these relationships where communication breaks down and attempts at conflict resolution fail to re-establish cordial interaction. In such cases it always pays to remain polite and not to jeopardise future relations unnecessarily (hence Figure 4.1 on p.58). The threat that breakdowns in communications poses is significant and even communities with extremely positive internal relationships can find their Plan scuppered by negative external ones. For that reason we also dedicate a section to where relationships run into difficulty in Chapter 6 (see Section 3).

The Local Planning Authority

Research shows that the relationship between the community and the Local Planning Authority is commonly the most important relationship to develop and maintain. The LPA must fulfil a series of legislative duties, including taking decisions at key stages in the process, and they also have a 'duty to support'. The specific requirements of the 'duty to support' are not explicitly articulated and each LPA has to determine the support they can provide. National Planning Practice Guidance (NPPG) acts as a steer here, exhorting Local Authorities to:

- Be proactive in providing information to communities about Neighbourhood Planning;
- Fulfil their duties and take decisions as soon as possible, and within statutory time periods where these apply;

- Set out a clear and transparent decision-making timetable and share this with communities engaged in Neighbourhood Planning;
- Constructively engage with the community throughout the process including when considering the recommendations of the independent examiner.

From the community perspective, support from the LPA is necessary and relates to four key elements: *resources and knowledge*; *evidence*; *alignment* with higher level policy; and adherence to the regulations. It is also worth highlighting that planning activity operates in a frequently changing environment, with policy and regulations being amended over time. Having institutional support is therefore important to maximise the chances of the Plan being robust and standing the test of time.

Despite the important role of the LPA, it has become clear that their support and willingness to engage fully with Neighbourhood Planning has been variable. There are a number of reasons for this: availability of resources, broader commitments and priorities (for example, the status of the Local Plan), their consideration of the value of Neighbourhood Planning and, in some cases, concerns about the impact of Neighbourhood Planning on their ability to deliver strategic planning. In some cases the LPA may have limited knowledge and experience of Neighbourhood Planning and may be on as much of a learning curve as the community. While this does not absolve them of their responsibilities and duties, time and patience may be required as the Local Planning Authority familiarises itself with the processes, regulations and intricacies of Neighbourhood Planning.

Details of the assistance the LPA can provide may be found in their Statement of Community Involvement, which should be publicly available (for example on their website). It is important for communities to have an open conversation with their Local Authority at the beginning of the Neighbourhood Planning process, to understand what support they can offer and when (including, for example, turn-around times for advice and whether there is a timetable to be followed e.g. scheduled meetings for decisions). As introduced in Section 4.2, it may be beneficial to consider formalising any relationship with the Local Planning Authority through a Memorandum of Understanding that can outline the level of support the LPA can and will provide, and in turn what they expect from the NP Steering Group.

Advice received may be formal or informal and groups would be well advised to ensure that interactions with LPA officers are undertaken knowing what inputs are intended to assist in an 'informal' way, and what constitutes formal advice that may impact on the success or speed of the Plan. Seek clarity with officers on this if in doubt and generally organise this through the Memorandum of Understanding (MoU) if you develop one i.e. with a section on communications.

In the same way that central government and third-party organisations have guidelines and processes that need to be followed, so will the LPA – templates or guidance documents e.g. Area and Forum application forms, Strategic Environmental Assessment templates, Housing Needs Assessment, site assessment forms or other specific things they require from the Steering Group or they prefer is used. It is important to discuss these with the LA at an early stage to avoid surprises later.

Consultants

Research has confirmed that the majority of groups appoint consultants for at least part of the work involved in preparing a Neighbourhood Plan. This can be expensive and mapping out skill sets within the community and matching these to tasks can maximise the utility of consultancy input (or preclude or reduce consultant inputs). This can also be done with reference to the type, level and timing of support that you can reasonably expect both from the LPA and from within the community or network on a *pro bono* or voluntary basis. This process will help you to identify and narrow down when particular assistance is needed and the type of support required.

Key points to consider when employing consultants:
- Be clear on the support and assistance required. Consultancy input can vary from supporting and advising groups on all

aspects of Plan development to focusing specifically on the technical aspects e.g. Strategic Environmental Assessment, Sustainability Appraisal and policy writing (this has been shown to be most useful in Neighbourhood Planning evaluation research);

- Decide on the type of relationship and level of involvement e.g. hand-holding through the process, production of bespoke pieces of work or an advisory role;
- Decide who to appoint – consultant services vary and their skills and ways of working need to match the support and assistance required by the group. It may be useful to speak to neighbouring groups, or the Local Planning Authority, and ask for their advice. The Royal Town Planning Institute (RTPI) maintains a list of Independent Consultants if an expertise in planning is required;
- Develop a clear written brief that explains the advice sought, timescales and indication of budget. This can be used as a basis for tender;
- Ensure that non-technical executive summaries are included in any technical documents procured – this will help to ensure citizen-planners understand the key findings;
- Avoid being beholden to the consultant. Neighbourhood Planning is ultimately 'community-led' which means the Plan will exist beyond the plan-making process. Therefore the knowledge and understanding of your area that you have gained as you go along sets you up for being a citizen-planner and can provide important identity and value to the final Plan.

If you are more prepared and aware of issues then you will be better able to use consultants effectively and assess whether you need to use them at all. Equally you may wish to appoint different consultants to assist you at the different stages or for discrete tasks (see Chapter 5).

Developers and landowners

A Neighbourhood Plan is a statutory land-use document that will be used in the determination of planning applications submitted by developers. In essence, developers will therefore be responsible for delivering the vision for the community and it is advised that communities engage openly and transparently with them as the Plan progresses. This will help them to understand what is hoped to be achieved and communities to understand if what they are proposing is deliverable and likely to be implemented over the Plan period. The starting point for many groups who are allocating sites for development is to organise a 'call for sites'. This provides the opportunity for those with land in the area to submit details of their land interest, any constraints to development and details of their preferred land use (this can be broad and include housing, employment, retail, community facilities or open space). The sites submitted as part of this process then can be assessed for inclusion as allocations in the Neighbourhood Plan (see also Chapter 5).

Engaging with developers and landowners does not mean that all matters will be agreed on and objections may be submitted during the consultation period as they seek to advance their interests. Furthermore, despite a Steering Group engaging with developers, as the Neighbourhood Plan progresses some may seek to subvert the process by submitting a planning application before the Plan is 'made'. Unfortunately this is a legitimate action and the Local Plan policies act as the prime factor in decision-making where this prevails.

Example 4.3   **Engaging with Developers**

Uppingham Town Council, Rutland, and Henfield Parish Council, Horsham, have both actively engaged with developers. Uppingham organised a 'developer' day and Henfield invited developers to attend a public meeting and give a site presentation. This provided the opportunity for developers to put forward their proposals and answer any questions from the community.

Oakley and Deane Parish, Basingstoke and Deane (Hampshire) decided to work with developers and inform them of how the Neighbourhood Plan would impact on site size and location as they were focusing on smaller sites across the parish. It was important the Local Planning Authority was supportive so that developers understood that the policy would be applied in decision-making.

Planning Aid England has produced a document entitled
'How to work with landowners and developers' and a case study
of West Hoathly Neighbourhood Plan which provides further
information and advice on this topic area is included.

When engaging with developers and landowners it is important
that the wider community is kept informed and conflicts of
interest are avoided (see above). This will help to ensure
openness, transparency and confidence in the process. Finally
in common with LPA officers, the development industry is a key
user of Plans and clarity and precision will be paramount. The
consequences of poorly crafted policy is to diminish its value or
even to invite legal challenge.

Central Government
As discussed in Chapters 2 and 3, Neighbourhood Planning is one
tier of the planning system and will be affected by wider policy
changes. Hence, although citizen-planners are unlikely to have
a direct relationship with Central Government, they will be
affected by policy decisions and, most directly, changes to the
Neighbourhood Planning regulations made there. Since its
introduction a number of changes have been made to speed up
and simplify the process and the LPA should be able to advise
you on any implications. Beyond that it is important to keep a
watchful eye on changes by signing up to bulletins, for example,
'Notes on Neighbourhood Planning' published by the Ministry
of Housing, Communities and Local Government (MHCLG)
and the Locality newsletter (details are provided in Chapter 9,
Section 6).

4.5 Reflections
This chapter has explained the importance of developing and
managing relationships whilst preparing a Neighbourhood Plan.
Such a Plan is essentially co-produced and requires input,
support and collaboration with those within the community and
external bodies and stakeholders including the LPA consultants
and developers and landowners. Negotiation skills and an ability
to resolve conflict are central to managing these relations as

those engaging in the process often have different perceptions, understandings and interests. As has been discussed, appropriate measures need to be put in place to ensure due process is followed, conflicts of interest are avoided and transparency and openness maintained. This will enable interested parties to have confidence and to understand the decision-making process.

Relationships need to be maintained and developed as the Neighbourhood Plan is progressed with different inputs and skills required at different phases of Plan development. As we discuss in Chapter 5, a project plan can also help to align and manage the various inputs required and to maintain relationships with not only the wider community but also the Local Planning Authority and consultants. Once the Plan is 'made' further negotiation may be required as it will not necessarily form a stable and static document. Neighbourhood Planning fits within the broader planning framework and ongoing negotiation and conversations may be required as the policies are implemented and planning applications are determined.

Actions
In order to consolidate the coverage in this chapter, ensure that the Steering Group has looked at, or reflected on:

- Some examples where Neighbourhood Plan groups have developed good relations with other stakeholders;
- Issues or topics that are likely to create division or tension;
- Areas of common ground that can be agreed upon;
- Who should lead on maintaining the types of relations discussed across particular aspects of Neighbourhood Plan production.

Please do reflect on how relationships affect and require consideration through our lens of the *themes*, *resources* and *phases* of Neighbourhood Planning.

5.1 Introduction

This chapter sets out the formal stages of Neighbourhood Planning that communities must adhere to in order to complete a Neighbourhood Plan. We have superimposed those stages with our view of how citizen-planners need a 'phased' approach, which highlights the style, types of action and approach required. Many Neighbourhood Planning resources are structured using formal Neighbourhood Plan stages (i.e. designation, consultation, examination, referendum and so on). Here, we go further by explaining the process, in terms of four phases of Neighbourhood Planning: *preparation*, *drafting*, *finalisation* and *implementation* – each requiring different roles, skills and inputs from citizen-planners (see Figure 5.1, overleaf).

5.2 The stages and phases of Neighbourhood Planning

This chapter sets out how to approach a Neighbourhood Plan and what to look out for throughout the process, based on the experience of those who have already gone through it. A number of case studies and examples are provided to help illustrate various points across the stages involved. We hope to ensure that communities are well prepared before embarking on the Plan, in terms of what to expect and the mindset required in the various phases of the project.

The overarching phases involve: *preparation* and getting set up; *drafting* i.e. the core steps in producing the draft Plan; *finalisation* featuring getting it past examination and referendum; and the 'post-planning' phase of *implementation* where the Plan should come alive and shape outcomes in the neighbourhood. The early preparation phases are frequently underplayed in existing advice and guidance but experience shows that they are very important. In reality of course the implementation phase loops back to preparation as a Plan is refreshed or a new Plan begins its lifecycle. We believe this is a helpful way of thinking about Neighbourhood Plan production, allowing the process to be considered as fluid and iterative, rather than solely as a series of consecutive steps that must be followed. In fact, like all processes involving people and institutions, the realities are much messier than merely completing preset 'stages' in a clear or linear fashion.

The four phases shown in Figure 5.1 also reveal the mindsets required by citizen-planners and the key tasks involved that will be encountered at each of the formal stages (see Example 5.1, overleaf).

The four phases of Neighbourhood Planning

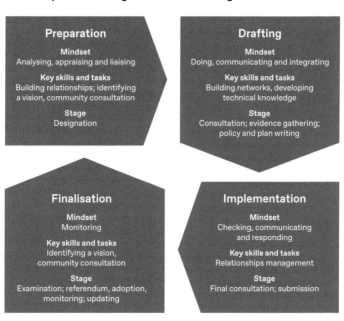

Figure 5.1

Figure 5.1 also indicates some of the necessary skills for effective Neighbourhood Planning across the phases (and formal stages of Plan production). Bearing in mind our guiding themes of *negotiation, integration* and *possibility*, it is apparent that certain types of skills and resources will be useful across those phases. These could be *technical skills and knowledge, project management, community engagement, mediation and relationship management*. The resources that are needed therefore suggest themselves as the following categories: *Money, Time, Knowledge, Influence* and *Partners*. The trick is to identify the skills and know-how needed across the different phases of plan-making – allied to the resources needed and available. Consider developing a 'plan for the Plan', which may involve shaping the vision then working backwards to think about resource elements and combinations likely to be required.

The formal stages involved in the Neighbourhood Planning process are detailed and explained in the NPPG and via existing advice (see Chapter 9, Sections 1 and 3). In Example 5.1, overleaf, we set out a breakdown of the stages and the constituent steps, which adds somewhat to the official and arguably simplistic versions available.

Formal governmental advice tends to focus on the 'middle' phases of drafting and finalisation and portrays very little about the early phase (preparation) and later phase (implementation). Indeed the regulatory stages underplay the actual steps that groups and their partners need to work through – what we refer to here as 'baby steps' or steps that feature at the different stages. This more detailed breakdown may assist citizen-planners to help think through their project plan and to consider what is required in terms of capacity, learning, information, technique/ expertise and partnering at each step in Plan preparation. Many of these steps involve numerous specific tasks, some of which fall on partner organisations, including the Local Planning Authority and on occasion input from consultants, and of course views derived from the wider community. This enriched set of steps is based on actual experience.

Example 5.1 ## The formal stages of Neighbourhood Planning (and 'baby steps') set against our 'four-phase thinking'

Phase 1 – Preparation [see Chapter 5, Section 3]
1 Consider the options – why a Neighbourhood Plan?
2 Learn about Neighbourhood Planning in overview
3 Initiate a project plan (and associated action plan)
4 Form a Steering Group/working groups and if in a non-Parished area begin to scope the membership of the Neighbourhood Forum
5 Designate the Neighbourhood Area (Formal Stage)
6 Designate the Neighbourhood Forum (Formal Stage)
7 Develop a Memorandum of Understanding with the Local Planning Authority

Phase 2 – Drafting [see Chapter 5, Section 4]
1 Consultation and community engagement (including preparing the Consultation Statement) (will need to be evidenced later)
2 Evidence gathering (evidence is needed to justify the policies)
3 Developing policies and projects (including preparing the Basic Conditions Statement)
4 Strategic Environmental Assessment (necessary in some circumstances e.g. if sites are to be allocated for development)

Phase 3 – Finalisation [see Chapter 5, Section 5]
1 Navigate regulations
2 Submit the Plan for examination
3 Appoint examiner (Formal Stage)
4 Examination (Formal Stage)
5 Neighbourhood Referendum (Formal Stage)

Phase 4 – Implementation [see Chapter 5, Section 6]
1 Plan is 'made', adopted by the Local Authority (Formal Stage)
2 Use the Plan – commenting on planning applications
3 Monitor, review and modify
4 Spin-off' and wider community benefits
6 Think about issues arising and prepare the ground for a refreshed Plan

Explaining these phases in more detail below, we focus on instances where existing advice is lacking, or where specific issues have been encountered by participating communities. We also provide a signpost to references and additional resources that are germane to the relevant stage.

—

5.3 Preparation

This requires a mindset that brings to the fore appraisal of the tools available, the issues to be tackled and the building of necessary support. Developing relations in this phase is critical to success and creating the conditions conducive to making good and robust decisions throughout the process. The early 'baby steps' therefore involve undertaking groundwork about planning and Neighbourhood Planning (which may include reading this book!). Thereafter some form of project planning will minimise the likelihood of wrong steps further down the line. The preparation stage should also involve assessing whether Neighbourhood Planning is the most appropriate tool for the community, and liaising with stakeholders in and beyond the neighbourhood.

Is it the right tool?

Alternative tools are available and a basic scan of these alternatives should be carried out very early; considering the options and how they apply to your circumstances could really help concentrate the mind about what the Neighbourhood Plan should focus on or whether other tools can achieve some or all of the goals that the Steering Group thought a Neighbourhood Plan could enable. A quick look at the Glossary (the asterisked Alternative Planning Tools) and the comments set out in Chapter 7 will help, as well as the items in Chapter 9, Section 4 for a deeper exploration.

Project planning

Research shows the average time taken to produce a Neighbourhood Plan is around two and a half years. This is the time typically taken *after* area designation to reach the final referendum stage – with many finding the process altogether quite complex and pretty burdensome. Our assessment is that around three years is a most likely timeframe until referendum (not allowing for some significant delay factor).

The importance of effective project planning cannot be underestimated as it will help to make the process as manageable, efficient and effective as possible. Project planning is a method of identifying and mapping out the specific tasks, resource requirements and time needed to deliver a project. It can also help groups to allocate tasks and roles and manage the relationship with others involved in the process (including the wider community, consultants and the LPA). There is a wealth of resources and templates available to assist groups including the *Resource for Neighbourhood Planning: Putting the Pieces Together* published by Planning Aid England.

The project planning stage can be broken down further in order to highlight key inputs and relationships, for example, to:

- Emphasise and identify the relationship(s) with the Local Planning Authority; a Steering Group may wish to consider having a Memorandum of Understanding (as discussed in Chapter 4, Section 4);
- Develop appropriate mechanisms to split the workload e.g. set up defined working groups;
- Identify when particular assistance is needed and the type of support required, for example, consultancy input, *pro bono* advice and assistance or input from the wider community.

Getting started and building support

The first statutory stage involved in producing a Plan is for the Neighbourhood Area to be designated and in non-Parished areas for a 'Qualifying Body' (i.e. a Neighbourhood Forum) to be established. The Neighbourhood Area is the territory over which the Plan's policies have effect and it can only be covered by one Neighbourhood Plan. It is possible for the Area to cut across boundaries or multiple parishes to combine to form a single Plan Area, as in, for example, Upper Eden, Cumbria. In Bishop Stortford, Hertfordshire the Plan covers part of a parish. Where appropriate, a Neighbourhood Area can also bridge more than one Local Authority boundary.

These stages are important not only in 'process' terms but also in building up support and relationships with the wider community. It is acknowledged that Plans are, by necessity, authored by a small group of people, however they should be owned and visible to the wider community and reflect their views and experiences (as far as possible). After all they will be voting on it at the referendum.

5.4 Drafting

By this stage you have decided to proceed with a Neighbourhood Plan and you may well have developed a working relationship with the LPA and set up a working group. Now the work in actually drawing together views and existing evidence really begins. This is the main phase of preparing the Neighbourhood Plans and where the bulk of the work is done. We focus on three main activities: community engagement and consultation; gathering evidence; and developing the policies (and projects). These should be viewed in an iterative way rather than forming distinct or discrete activities.

Community engagement and consultation

There is overlap between the 'preparation' phase and 'drafting the plan' with regard to community engagement and consultation. As discussed in Chapter 1, the Plan needs to reflect the views of the community without trampling on pre-existing or otherwise fundamental aspirations of the community that have been borne out by evidence. There is potential in Neighbourhood Planning to be innovative and to integrate the Plan responsibly with regional, local or indeed national needs (see Chapter 7).

Ongoing engagement and consultation is therefore essential and should not be limited to the two statutory consultation phases (i.e. consultation on the Pre-Submission 'Regulation 14' and Publicity 'Regulation 16') stages of the Plan. Note that citizen-planners will need to read and understand the formal stages of Neighbourhood Planning in the regulations and see Chapter 6). The earlier the wider community knows about the emerging Plan the better. Their involvement is vital to the democratic legitimacy of the process and will ultimately influence the quality of the Plan. Further information on intra-community relationships can be found in Chapter 4. The extent and effectiveness of community engagement will be considered by

the examiner and may result in a recommendation that the
Plan does not proceed to referendum (see Example 5.2).

Example 5.2 **Reflecting the views of the community**
Sandon Burston Neighbourhood Plan, Staffordshire

Here the examiner concluded that public consultation was
'not robust' as:

> *'there is evidence to demonstrate that the*
> *Neighbourhood Plan fails to reflect the views of*
> *local people...consequently, I cannot conclude*
> *that the Neighbourhood Plan reflects a shared*
> *vision for the neighbourhood area'.*

In this regard, the Neighbourhood Plan did not meet the
Basic Conditions as it did not have regard to national policy
under the then applicable NPPF (2012: Paragraphs 193–184).

Ensuring that the Plan is grounded in community views at an
early stage is central to the Plan's resilience. In practice this
means identifying the core issues of concern to the whole
community at an early stage and allowing these to help shape
the Plan, the specific topics you wish to focus on and the key
priorities for the area. The community should also be involved
in discussions on how particular issues could be addressed,
which could include, for example, the Local Green Spaces to be
protected or the priorities for green cycling and walking links
(see Figure 5.1).

← Collective
mapping:
priorities for
green walking
and cycling
links, with a
range of project
budgets.

→ Engagement
on the
Neighbourhood
Plan.

Having identified the issues of importance, communities should then assess whether there is corroborating evidence that justifies or reflects attitudes and preferences and whether the issue is adequately addressed in the Local Plan or through National Policy. If it is not, then locally distinctive policies that add value may be appropriate to include in the Plan. Care should be taken not to simply repeat national or local policies as this may result in not only duplication of effort but potential for unintended consequences such as policy dilution. Furthermore, such policies could be deleted by the independent examiner. Our advice is always seek to add value or specificity to suit local need or circumstance.

Early community consultation will enable communities to develop a clear vision of how the area is to develop over the Plan period. This should be locally distinctive, framed positively and tell a story about how the area is expected to change. Developing a narrative in this sense can be useful in convincing other stakeholders of the value of the Plan, which speaks to the idea of Neighbourhood Planning as negotiative. It should be included in the Neighbourhood Plan alongside a series of objectives that will help to deliver the vision. The vision and objectives form the spine of the Plan and each policy should relate to one (or more) of the

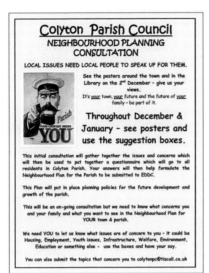

← Engagement on the Neighbourhood Plan, Colyton Neighbourhood Plan, Devon.

objectives. This is useful for Planning Policy officers and those drawing on the Plan for decision-making purposes. This helps those parties to understand the intention behind the policies and therefore assist in their interpretation and implementation.

There are a range of methods and techniques that can be adopted to engage with the community and specific attention should be paid to engaging with 'hard to reach' groups, particularly those who are often overlooked by participatory processes, including the elderly, the young, single parents and ethnic minority groups.

Groups have adopted a range of creative measures to engage with the community and to seek inclusivity of process, including:

- Considering the timings of meetings and consultation events;
- Translating information about the Plan into different languages to reflect the profile of the community;
- Holding specific events for children and young people, for example, a competition to design the Neighbourhood Plan logo has been used, and one group organised a 'rave' for young people to attend;

- Using a range of consultation techniques in order to engage with people of all ages (e.g. setting up a bespoke Facebook account and other social media channels to engage with the younger generation), however, this should not replace traditional consultation methods such as household questionnaires and articles/adverts in local publications. Methods adopted by groups include 'wish-carts' and 'wishing trees' for people to add their ideas and preferences (e.g. Old Market Quarter, Bristol), photography competitions (e.g. Weedon Bec, Daventry) and street fairs (e.g. BBEST Neighbourhood Forum, Sheffield);
- Extending the statutory consultation periods beyond six weeks if it falls over a holiday period (e.g. Christmas or summer holidays);
- Organising specific events to engage with the business community (e.g. breakfast seminars; business surveys);
- Engaging with developers and landowners who have an interest in land within the Neighbourhood Area (e.g. organise developer drop-in sessions and/or presentation events; see Example 4.3 on p.68).

It is advisable to record all the engagement and consultation events and techniques adopted as the Plan is developed. This information will need to be included in the Consultation Statement that is submitted for examination alongside the draft Neighbourhood Plan. The Consultation Statement is your opportunity to explain and demonstrate how engagement with your community and others has shaped the development of your Neighbourhood Plan and it must include the following:

- Details of the persons and bodies who were consulted about the proposed Neighbourhood Plan;
- An explanation of how they were consulted;
- A summary of the main issues and concerns raised by the persons consulted;
- A description of how these issues and concerns have been considered and, where relevant, addressed in the proposed Neighbourhood Plan.

MALBOROUGH NEIGHBOURHOOD PLAN

DROP IN SESSION

For Malborough's parishioners

CONSULTATION

SITE OPTIONS

FOR HOUSING

4pm – 8pm All Saints Church

MONDAY, MARCH 7th 2016

YOUR FUTURE
YOUR VOICE
YOUR PLAN

← Drop-in consultation on-site options for housing, Malborough Neighbourhood Plan, Wiltshire.

This information should be provided in a comprehensive way to enable the wider community and those with an interest in the Plan to understand the process that has been followed; and how it has been amended throughout the process to take on board the comments raised. It is an important piece of evidence and will be considered as part of the examination process. What we are saying is that the way engagement is carried out is important (see Example 5.3, below).

Example 5.3 **Importance of community engagement and consultation Burpham Neighbourhood Plan, Surrey**

Here the examiner raised concerns over the level of engagement in the Neighbourhood Plan and the nature of consultation. Issues raised included: the opportunities provided for those without a computer to engage in the process; whether the requirement had been made to bring the Plan to the attention of those who work or do business in the area; whether methods were taken to inform residents of the consultation e.g. placing of posters of leaflets in a prominent position indicating where the plan can be inspected; and that there was no mention of any measures taken to engage with particular groups of the population, such as young people or the elderly. The consultation statement was also criticised as follows:

> The response to comments is very brief and uninformative in many cases, simply stating noted or amended. In relation to critical comments...there is little or no explanation of why the comments are not accepted, and responses are defensive, avoiding addressing the main issue.

The examiner concluded that the:

> programme of consultation was not as far reaching or effective as it could have been. The reluctance to take on board some of the suggestions made during consultation has consequences for my consideration of individual policies later in this report'. The Plan would have 'benefitted substantially' from more thorough consultation and 'it would have had wider ownership and the policies would have been more effectively evaluated and refined with the input of a wider cross section of the community.'

Gathering evidence

A strong evidence base forms the foundation of a Neighbourhood Plan. The NPPG (para 40; Reference ID: 41-040-20160211) states that there is no 'tick box' list of evidence required. However, a proportionate, robust evidence base should support the choices made and the approach taken. The evidence should be drawn upon to explain succinctly the intention and rationale of the policies with a summary of the evidence relevant to support each policy (see Example 5.4, below). Where necessary, the reader should also be directed to a more comprehensive evidence base as required (for example, some groups have produced helpful 'topic papers' that sit alongside the Plan).

Example 5.4   **Evidence to justify Neighbourhood Plan policies Burpham Neighbourhood Plan, Surrey**

This example is drawn from Burpham Neighbourhood Plan, Surrey (also Example 5.3) which passed examination but was substantially modified, as explained by the examiner:

> While substantial factual evidence has been presented,
> in many cases it is not clear how this has been used in the
> formulation of policies. The absence of justification has
> meant that it has been necessary for me to suggest a large
> number of modifications and the deletion of several
> policies in order for the Plan to meet the Basic Conditions...
> Clear and robust reasoning based on the views expressed
> by the community, the evidence available to the forum and
> national policy and guidance would have resulted in more
> defensible and effective policies.

The evidence collected will be context- and Plan-specific –
while you may wish to have a look at the policies in other 'made'
Neighbourhood Plans for inspiration it is important that you do
not just copy them. Ensure the policy is relevant to the particular
locality and that appropriate and robust evidence is present to
substantiate the policy. It is of course sensible to test the
language used and this can be achieved by reviewing the specific
wording of policies in adopted Local Plans (these will have been
subject to scrutiny and tested at their own examination).

Furthermore, as discussed in the previous section,
community views do not in themselves constitute 'evidence',
however, they can provide a steer on the areas and topics for
which evidence should be gathered. One way of thinking about
this is that community views in and of themselves are likely to
be 'evidence'. These issues may show up how a preference or
need has been voiced and then evidence will be applied or
commissioned that acts to support or otherwise adjust such
views. The Steering Group will need to be mindful of the iterative
aspect of such work and again relationship management plays a
role here too (see Chapter 4). There are a number of sources of
evidence and Planning Aid England has produced a diagram
of 'sources of data and statistics' which you may find useful
(see Chapter 9, Section 5).

For most groups it is worthwhile to discuss evidence
requirements with the LPA early on in the process. The NPPG
(para 40; Reference ID: 41-040-20160211) states that a Local
Planning Authority 'should share relevant evidence, including
that gathered to support its own plan-making with a Qualifying
Body with the NPPF also providing a useful overview of the types

of evidence that the LPA may have collected. Things to consider and discuss with the LPA are whether the information is available at an appropriate geographical scale, if it is considered up-to-date and whether it has been tested through examination (if not, then it may be subject to change).

Groups should also take the opportunity to discuss the Local Plan strategy for their area and the strategic policies that are of relevance. This is important as some Local Planning Authorities identify a specific 'housing target' for named settlements or an overall target that Neighbourhood Plans across the district or unitary area should deliver. This may influence the scope, scale and evidence required to support the policies and approach in the Plan. Similarly, some issues may be addressed at a strategic level, and not at a neighbourhood level, which means further evidence will not usually be required. This is often the case for affordable housing policies and thresholds that are based on an assessment of viability set across the Local Authority area.

The NPPF and NPPG also provide a steer on evidence requirements for particular policy areas commonly included in Neighbourhood Plans. For example, many groups decide to allocate land for housing in their Neighbourhood Plan and the NPPG (para 9; Reference ID: 41-009-20160211) states that 'up-to-date housing needs evidence is relevant to the question of whether a housing supply policy in a Neighbourhood Plan or Order contributes to the achievement of Sustainable Development'. This information may be available from the Local Authority. If not, it may need to be commissioned from consultants.

As of 2018, amended national policy (NPPF) suggests that LPAs provide Steering Groups with a housing needs figure that will help to provide further certainty. As with any change in National Policy there will be a period of transition as this approach is rolled out and adopted across the board. Steering Groups will need to be mindful of how such changes are applied locally or whether further alterations to this aspect of local- and neighbourhood-scale planning unfold. A number of groups have had proposed Local Green Space designations deleted at the examination as they did not meet the criteria set out in the NPPF. The NPPF (2012) was clear that 'the designation should only be used where the green space is in reasonably close proximity to the community it serves; is demonstrably special to a local community and holds a particular local significance, and is local in character and not an extensive tract of land' (NPPG, para 76; Reference ID: 41-076-20140306). Groups will therefore need to collect evidence to demonstrate that the proposed Local Green Space meets each of the criteria.

As well as needing evidence to support proposed allocations and policies, robust evidence is also required to support decisions that have been made and to ensure transparency of process. For example, if allocating sites for development (including housing sites), an appraisal of options and an assessment of individual sites against clearly identified criteria should be carried out. It is often the case that there is more than one approach or method that can be adopted. This is fine in principle but there is a need to explain which method the group adopted and why. There are lots of examples out there and templates that can be used as a guide. However, they are exactly that – a guide – and may need to be modified in order to reflect specific local circumstances.

—

Example 5.5   **Evidence to justify Neighbourhood Plan policies Weedon Bec Neighbourhood Plan, Northamptonshire**

This extract from the examiner's report explains why the Plan was failed at examination:

> The site allocations...do not sufficiently take account of national policy and guidance as their selection is not underpinned by any discussion or use of the latest evidence of housing need or any persuasive justification or any proportionate or robust evidence. Whilst the sites have been appraised, there is a lack of apparent transparency in the selection of sites.

Having canvassed opinion and sought out issues of concern or preferences, the development of a robust evidence base is critical as it forms a fundamental part of the process of formulating, and deciding whether or not to include, a policy or policies in the Plan.

Developing policies (and projects)

Neighbourhood Plan policies provide the basis for the determination of planning applications and they must relate to the development and use of land. There is no set list of policies that should be included within a Plan, and each Plan should be locally distinctive and seek to address the particular issues in the locality. Plans produced to date vary considerably in scope with the number of policies ranging from as few as two to over a hundred. The NPPG advises that:

> a policy in a Neighbourhood Plan should be clear and unambiguous. It should be drafted with sufficient clarity that a decision-maker can apply it consistently and with confidence when determining planning applications. It should be concise, precise and supported by appropriate evidence, reflecting and responding to both the context and the characteristics of the area (NPPG, para 41; Reference ID: 41-041-20140306)

The planning policies should be easily identifiable within the Neighbourhood Plan and numbered in a logical manner to aid navigation by the reader. The following should be considered:

- The Basic Conditions as you develop the policies, particularly whether they are in general conformity with the strategic policies in the adopted Local Plan. Furthermore, there are a number of topics that cannot be addressed, such as minerals, waste or nationally significant infrastructure;
- The policies must be *positively prepared*, e.g. focus on what will be permitted and encouraged as opposed to what will be opposed/not allowed;
- The policies must be supported by *robust evidence* (see Chapter 5, Section 4) and not just based on local opinion – you should direct the reader to the relevant evidence base;
- Ensure adequate explanation of the *policy intent* is provided in the supporting text, which sits either above or below the policy, as this will help a decision-maker to interpret the policy as intended;

- The policies should help to deliver the *vision and the objectives* of the Plan and tell a story as to how the community will develop in the future;
- *Non-land-use policies should be clearly separated* from the land-use planning policies, for example, be included within an appendix or a separate section of the Plan. These will not be tested at examination and do not form part of the statutory Planning Policy document. For some communities it may be appropriate for these projects and proposals to then be incorporated into an action plan document or a community plan to be taken forward by the Parish or Town Council and community outside of the mainstream planning system (for further information see Chapter 7);
- The Policies must be *deliverable* and be capable of being delivered within the timeframe of the Plan. Furthermore, they must also only relate to proposals within the designated Neighbourhood Plan area;
- *Clarity* – the policies need to be specific and clear. The policies that appear in the final Plan are implemented by others and no room for misapplication should be left;
- *Duplication should be avoided* – there is no need to include a policy on every issue within the Neighbourhood Area as many will be adequately addressed by national policy or the Local Plan.

It is advisable to engage with the LPA as the Plans and policies are prepared. They should provide constructive comments on an emerging Plan and discuss the contents of any supporting documents (see NPPG on Neighbourhood Planning, para 67; Reference ID: 41-067-20140306). Based on their technical experience and knowledge of the broader planning context, including the NPPF and the Local Plan, the LPA should be able to provide advice on whether the emerging Plan meets the Basic Conditions, highlight any potential difficulties and in some cases propose ways in which the Plan and the draft policies could be strengthened.

In addition, some groups decide to appoint an external independent advisor to produce a 'health check' of the Plan, which involves proofing the Plan against the types of tests we have outlined. Comments on the policies may also be received as part of the pre-submission consultation, including representations from formal consultation bodies (further information on the pre-submission publicity and consultation, including the consultation bodies, can be found in the NPPG) and local interest groups. The involvement and engagement of these bodies early on can alert you to other sources of evidence and they can often provide valuable insight and support.

Once feedback to the consultation is provided the community should respond in a considered way. Often comments received can help to strengthen the Plan. The Consultation Statement must explain and demonstrate how engagement with your community and others has shaped the development of your Neighbourhood Plan (see Chapter 5, Section 3).

Alongside preparing the Plan, the group must compile a Basic Conditions Statement that needs to be submitted alongside the Neighbourhood Plan and the Consultation Statement. This needs to set out how the Neighbourhood Plan meets the requirements of each Basic Condition and other legal tests. It is an important document and enables the group to explain to the examiner and the Local Planning Authority how the Plan meets the legal tests and therefore why it should proceed to referendum. It is advisable that the Basic Conditions Statement is prepared alongside the Plan as it is created, as this will help groups to assess whether the policies being drafted are suitable and will pass the required tests.

Strategic Environmental Assessment

A Neighbourhood Plan may require a Strategic Environmental Assessment (SEA, see Glossary) if it is likely to have a significant effect on the environment. This may be the case, for example, where a Plan allocates land for development. A draft Plan should be assessed to determine whether the Plan is 'likely to have significant' environmental effects (this is commonly referred to as a 'screening' assessment, see Example 5.6) and if such a process is not adequate the Plan is open to challenge (see Chapter 6, Section 4 and Example 6.2).

You should seek the advice of your LPA at the early stages of Plan production on SEA. Planning Practice Guidance covering Strategic Environmental Assessment and Sustainability Appraisal advises that 'the Local Planning Authority, as part of its duty to advise or assist, should consider putting in place processes to determine whether the proposed Neighbourhood Plan will require a strategic environmental assessment'. The Qualifying Body (in effect the Steering Group) 'should work with the Local Planning Authority to be sure that the Authority has the information it needs' (NPPG, para 28; Reference ID: 11-028-20150209).

If the 'screening' assessment identifies likely significant effects, an environmental report must then be prepared in accordance with the Environmental Assessment of Plans and Programmes Regulations 2004 and submitted as part of the Neighbourhood Plan examination process. The NPPG coverage on SEA requirements for Neighbourhood Plans also advises that 'the processes for gathering evidence for the environmental report and for producing the draft Neighbourhood Plan can be integrated, and to allow the assessment process to inform the choices being made in the plan' (NPPG, para 29; Reference ID: 11-029-20150209). It is imperative that the environmental report considers reasonable alternatives that are realistic options whilst developing the Plan.

If the 'screening' opinion determines that an environmental assessment is not required then a statement of the reasons for the determination should be prepared and submitted with the Neighbourhood Plan and made available to the independent examiner (NPPG, para 28; Reference ID: 41-028-20140306). One of the Basic Conditions that will be tested by the independent examiner is whether the making of the Neighbourhood Plan is compatible with European Union obligations (including under the Strategic Environmental Assessment Directive). You must meet the requirements of the Environmental Assessment of Plans and Programmes Regulations 2004, including the consultation requirements.

Example 5.6 **Meeting the requirements of the SEA Directive**
Loxwood Neighbourhood Plan, West Sussex

Following an independent examination the Plan was subject to
a legal challenge around the failure of the District Council to
carry out a legally compliant screening opinion to determine
whether a Strategic Environmental Assessment of the Plan was
required. A legally compliant screening opinion was thus carried
out, however, this meant the Plan had to be resubmitted for
consultation and led to a re-examination which produced a
lengthy delay.

5.5 Finalisation

The penultimate phase is where the effort to pull the Plan
together is checked. We see value in the Steering Group reviewing
all the work done and thinking through how and whether the
Basic Conditions have been met. The phase culminates in
submitting the Plan for examination.

Navigating regulations

Due to the statutory processes involved in developing a
Neighbourhood Plan it is essential that the group learn to
effectively navigate the numerous regulatory requirements. In
some cases this can feel like jumping through hoops, however,
the process reflects the importance that will be placed on the
final document as once 'made' it forms part of the statutory
planning policy framework and due process must therefore be
followed. As discussed in Chapter 5, Section 2, project planning
is essential and can help to smooth the process and make it as
manageable, efficient and effective as possible.

Failure to follow the legislative requirements can lead to
challenges at examination, or potentially a legal challenge at the
High Court, or time delays as stages may have to be repeated.
For example, the pre-submission consultation will have to be
repeated if it does not last the statutory six weeks or if the
relevant consultation bodies are not consulted. It is also
important to consider the *outcomes* of the process; for example,
if the Plan is substantially modified following pre-submission
consultation then you may wish to consider undergoing a round
of further consultation before submission for examination. This

may help to ensure that all have had adequate opportunity to comment on the policies and proposals as the Plan has been prepared (and revised), which, as we have explained, is an important consideration at examination.

Independent examination

Once the draft Plan has been finalised it is submitted to the LPA for examination and the Local Planning Authority takes responsibility for the latter stages of the process. This includes responsibility for organising publicity on the Plan (a further six-week consultation period during which representations can be made), organising the examination, considering the examiners' recommendations and deciding whether to send the Plan to referendum. If it is a positive outcome at the examination then the LPA is also responsible for organising the referendum and the 'making' of the Plan.

As discussed, the Neighbourhood Plan itself, the Consultation Statement, the Basic Conditions Statement, either an environmental report or a statement of the reasons for the determination that an environmental assessment is not required in order to meet European Union obligations (see Chapter 5, Section 4 Strategic Environmental Assessment) and any supporting documents (for example, the evidence base or topic papers) must be submitted to the independent examiner. The independent examiner is appointed by the LPA, with the agreement of the Qualifying Body, and they must be 'appropriately qualified' and meet a number of basic requirements, i.e. that the examiner:

- Is independent of the Qualifying Body and the Local Planning Authority;
- Does not have an interest in any land that may be affected by the draft Order (the Plan);
- Has appropriate qualifications and experience.

It is expected that the examination of a draft Neighbourhood Plan will take the form of written representations (see Example 5.7). This means that the examiners will have to rely on the documents and evidence submitted to them and reaffirm the importance of the Basic Conditions Statement. National Planning Practice Guidance states that the Basic Conditions Statement is likely to be the main way that the group can seek to demonstrate that the draft Neighbourhood Plan meets the Basic Conditions (NPPG, para 68; Reference ID: 41-068-20140306). Furthermore, groups should ensure that evidence is there to substantiate the policies and it is easy for the examiner to find.

Example 5.7   **Informing the examiner**

We wrote a report on the basis of the Neighbourhood Planning officer's advice that there would be an oral hearing, but then there wasn't – if we'd have known we would have written more to defend our Plan, and the green gap policy in particular... he could only go on what we had written and on this basis proposed changes.
(Parker, Lynn and Wargent, 2017)

The role of the examination is to test whether the Plan meets a series of legislative requirements and the Basic Conditions. This means that the examiner will not be testing the Plan for soundness, its planning merits or other material considerations. It is a key stage in the process and a large proportion of Plans have been significantly modified following examination with amendments to policy wording, deletion of policies and the restructuring of the Plan document.

Having said all this the examiner's report is non-binding – it is up to the LPA to consider any recommendations and if necessary to modify the Plan to ensure it meets the Basic Conditions before allowing it to proceed to referendum. If possible, groups should seek to discuss the examiner's recommendations and proposed modifications with the LPA in order to ensure that, as far as possible, the Plan still reflects the communities' aspirations. In this respect two useful examples are worth considering. The first is Swanwick (Derbyshire), where the Plan was unsuccessful at referendum. The examiner recommended a series of modifications to the Plan that were accepted by the Local Planning Authority. However, those preparing the Plan, and the wider community, disagreed and actively campaigned for a 'no' vote as they argued that the revised Neighbourhood Plan no longer represented the aspirations of the community. The second is Littlehampton (West Sussex) where the referendum was postponed to allow additional time for the Local Planning Authority and the Neighbourhood Planning group to consider the examiner's recommendations and to pause, reflect and agree on the modifications to the Neighbourhood Plan. Clearly if such circumstances emerge there is a need to understand the reasons and each other's positions. This does not mean that there will be agreement but an open conversation will be useful and inform next steps.

Referendum

The community or neighbourhood referendum is a formal stage of Neighbourhood Planning. Responsibility for organising, and paying for, the referendum lies with the 'relevant council' (usually the lead LPA). They will make information about the referendum available to voters, however they are prohibited from publishing promotional material during the referendum period and there are restrictions on who can campaign. There may be some delay between finalising the Plan after examination and the date of the referendum. For example, the Council may decide to wait and hold the referendum at the same time as other elections (e.g. local elections), or on the same day as other Neighbourhood Plan referendums locally.

The outcome is decided by a simple majority (i.e. if more than 50% vote 'yes' then the Plan passes referendum). However, different rules apply in areas designated as Business Neighbourhood Areas, where two referendums are held: one for residents and one for businesses. If the situation arises where one referendum is successful and the other is not then the LPA makes the final decision on adoption (i.e. to 'make' the Plan). Further information on such Plans can be located in Chapter 9, Section 5.

Given the LA cannot publish promotional material during the referendum period, there are some sensitivities around campaigning for a particular outcome. Individuals or groups need to regard the general restrictions on referendum expenses and need to ensure that any publicity material is correctly attributed and factually correct. In some areas the referendums

→
Celebrating a
'yes' vote at
referendum –
Winslow
Neighbourhood
Plan,
Buckinghamshire.

have been very contentious with active 'yes' and 'no' campaigns. While this can be frustrating and emotions may be raised it is important to stick to the facts and to avoid publishing any defamatory material.

The majority of Neighbourhood Planning referendums are uncontroversial, and Plans typically pass with a high 'yes' vote. However there are exceptions to this rule, and some referendums do become highly charged political events. The good news is that in the course of preparing a Plan, citizen-planners will be aware of how contentious or not the vote can be, and are therefore forewarned. It is important to be aware that the Neighbourhood Plan sits within the wider framework of local planning, and may be tied up in local politics too. It may be useful therefore in the course of preparing the Plan for citizen-planners to be explicit to their own population about what a Neighbourhood Plan is (and what it is not). For example, that Plans must adhere to higher tier policy and cannot refute the Local Plan where it is in place.

One of the successes of Neighbourhood Planning to date has been its ability to integrate three forms of democracy in one process: the role of the LPA (steered through r*epresentative* democracy), the influence of the consultation process with the wider community (involving *participatory* democracy) and the final expression of community wishes through the referendum (*direct* democracy). In some ways, the referendum is a vote on the perceived legitimacy of the representative and participatory aspects of Plan production, as much as the content of the Plan itself. Therefore the more informed that the electorate (e.g. the community) are about the Neighbourhood Planning process, the better. Indeed some Steering Groups have provided literature to the community seeking to explain the process.

5.6 Implementation

The final phase is often overlooked by communities and yet is critical to the success of the Plan in terms of effecting change i.e. how it is actually used. Thus, the Plan will need to be formally adopted or 'made' by the LPA and then consideration of how planning officers and local councillors use it is important. After the dust has settled, the Steering Group should ensure that the existing 'network', formed to develop the Plan, is aware of changes and of the timeline for the medium-term to renew the Plan.

Making of the Plan and next steps

A Neighbourhood Plan comes into force as part of the statutory development plan once it has been approved at referendum. The LPA must then make the Plan within eight weeks of the referendum. Neighbourhood Planning bodies will be notified directly by the Local Planning Authority of any planning applications submitted within their designated Neighbourhood Plan area once the Plan passes examination. After the Plan has been made (and indeed to some extent prior to that, i.e. after Referendum) the Plan becomes 'material'. To ensure that the content is actually applied in decisions it will be important to represent and highlight the 'voice of the Plan' in planning applications – both those to be determined under 'delegated powers' and those that go to the Local Planning Authority Planning Committee for decision.

The Steering Group may wish to take the opportunity to comment on any planning applications and use the policies in the Neighbourhood Plan as part of their representations. Arrangements for implementing the Neighbourhood Plan should be considered early in the process as in many areas the Steering Group will disband once the Plan is 'made'. It then falls to the Qualifying Body to ensure the Plan is upheld (along with the LPA). This understanding of what happens to the Plan after being 'made' could form part of the terms of reference discussed in Chapter 4, Section 3. However it is impossible to predetermine how any given planning application will or should be viewed – the basis for the English planning system rests on that of discretion and each set of circumstances will differ. The judgement of the LPA will be nuanced and ultimately they will decide on a case-by-case basis with policy acting to help guide decisions rather than codify them.

As indicated above the community needs to understand that in large measure the power of implementation rests with the developers and the Local Planning Authority. As such the precision of the policy writing is critical and this has been a source of concern for many groups. As a result this aspect of Neighbourhood Planning has seen a significant role for consultancy assistance. Groups are advised to develop their understanding of the need for clear, concise and effective policy and how to craft this (see also Chapter 6, Section 4).

Reviewing the Plan

Once the Plan is 'made', or in many cases once the examination process has finished, the Steering Group will be able to take a well-earned break. However, considering the dynamic nature of the planning system it is unlikely that the Plan's policies will remain up-to-date and relevant for the whole Plan period. Thus, there will be a need for groups to keep their Plan under review and monitor its implementation – this responsibility will fall to the Qualifying Body (i.e. the Parish/Town Council where one exists) as opposed to the Steering Group, and in areas with a Neighbourhood Forum this may well require the Forum to apply for re-designation (the designation only lasts for five years).

There is no requirement to review or update a Neighbourhood Plan but there are several circumstances that may necessitate this: if the Neighbourhood Plan policies conflict or are otherwise superseded by policies in a Local Plan that is adopted after the making of the Neighbourhood Plan (as the more recent policy takes precedence), or due to broader policy changes (e.g. new regulations brought in by central government) or through a significant legal clarification. Some groups have opted for a 'refresh' after a few years, while others, if there has been more significant change, have opted to begin a new Plan. This may be a daunting prospect and research shows a certain amount of volunteer fatigue. However, in order to ensure the Plan policies remain relevant and part of the statutory development plan up-to-date policies are required. Further information on the process for modifying a Neighbourhood Plan can be found in the latest version of the NPPG.

Wider community benefits

Once the Neighbourhood Plan has been made it may form the basis for spin-off community projects or proposals. While the final Plan will contain the statutory planning policies a robust evidence base will have been gathered and community support will have been demonstrated. This may therefore provide a strong basis for additional funding and grants to be levered in to support the delivery of the broader Plan aspirations and to help deliver associated community projects. Further examples can be seen in Chapter 7, Section 2.

The process of producing a Neighbourhood Plan can involve a steep learning curve as expertise and knowledge is gathered along the way. Those involved, and to some extent the wider community, will have greater knowledge of the planning system and this will enable them to engage more effectively and constructively with future proposals in the area and to have a better understanding of community issues and what is of real importance to residents. This in itself can be invaluable.

5.7 Reflections

The stages and associated tasks involved in producing a Neighbourhood Plan can seem daunting. However, careful organisation and project planning will undoubtedly help groups to stay on track by identifying the specific tasks, resource requirements and time needed to deliver the project. As previously discussed, different skills and knowledge may be required at the various stages of Plan production and having a greater understanding, from the outset, about what is required at each stage can assist with the allocation of tasks and roles. This helps groups to manage the relationship with others involved in the process (including the wider community, consultants and the LPA).

When producing the Neighbourhood Plan it is essential to stay focused on what a Neighbourhood Plan is and what it can do. It is a statutory planning document that must include a series of clear, deliverable, implementable and focused land-use policies that are based on a robust evidence base. In addition to the requirements at each regulatory stage, the Plan must meet a series of Basic Conditions and it is essentially 'bounded' by higher tiers of planning policy. These serve not only to frame the Neighbourhood Planning process but also to enable groups to focus on the key issues facing their locality and to produce a locally distinctive Neighbourhood Plan that does not repeat national or local policy.

Chapter 4 has already focused on the key relationships involved in producing a Neighbourhood Plan, which can help you to navigate the process, and Chapter 7 introduces some reflective points on the issues raised in this chapter. As highlighted in previous chapters, keep in mind the key themes to ensure that the balance of *possibility*, *integration* and *negotiation* are maintained, alongside the *phase* and disposition implications and the resources that will be required.

Actions
In order to consolidate the coverage in this chapter ensure that that the Steering Group has understood or developed:

- The draft Neighbourhood Plan Plan (and revise it throughout);
- The available evidence that could be used to support the Plan and where gaps exist;
- The requirements necessary to meet the Basic Conditions

and in particular the form and content of the documents required (e.g. the Basic Conditions Statement and the Consultation Statement);

- The requirements and importance of meeting the SEA Directive;
- How best to shape and implement the first phase of Plan-making given the above.

Chapter 6

**Challenges in
Neighbourhood Planning**

6.1 Introduction

This chapter highlights common issues involved in both Neighbourhood Planning and participatory democracy more generally, drawing on the experiences of Neighbourhood Planning communities from across the country and from the extensive research literature in the participatory democracy field. Many of the challenges involved in Neighbourhood Planning are cross-cutting and so the chapter does not proceed sequentially by stage or phase (see Chapter 5) but groups the challenges involved across three themes: *support, translation* and *technicalities*. In concluding, this chapter reflects on the need simultaneously to recognise the processes involved in co-production (such as negotiation and integration) and the importance of firmly establishing the citizen-planner role within the wider planning system.

6.2 Overcoming challenges

During the process of producing a Plan multiple issues may arise that can, at times, make the process feel like an endurance test. By exploring these issues and making suggestions on how to overcome these challenges we hope that they can be avoided, minimised or at least prepared for. In this chapter, ideas about innovative planning and a more solutions-focused orientation are also provided. Here, the focus is on managing the process through possible crises, in terms of:

- The help and resources needed (*support*);

- Content and issues (*translation*);
- Meeting the required standards of a statutory planning document (*technicalities*).

The hurdles that are frequently encountered by Neighbourhood Planning groups and the precautions and solutions that citizen-planners can employ to insulate their Plan and minimise disruption to the plan-making process are far ranging. The previous chapters have emphasised the need to maintain positive open and reciprocal relationships with local stakeholders. This is important because the planning system is inherently political, with many different interests at play, which makes community-led planning a frequently challenging process. Maintaining the support of the community and other stakeholders, such as the LPA, can prove to be the difference between overcoming challenges and the challenges overcoming the Plan.

There may be significant roadblocks that present their own frustrations. These are typically caused by combinations of change, misunderstanding, gaps in evidence and the hurdles in the process, and can require editing or rethinks. Returning briefly to the three themes of this book, introduced in Chapter 1, many of these challenges reflect the need for communities both to *negotiate* between stakeholders and their interests and to translate (as part of the *integration* theme) the community's aspirations in order that they become part of the wider planning system (as highlighted in Chapter 3 and reprised in Chapter 8). Just as importantly, this maintains the idea of Neighbourhood Planning as a space of *possibility*. It is often necessary to overcome resistance to change and new ideas in order to establish local solutions and ensure 'value added', which can benefit the community through a Neighbourhood Plan. Thus retaining a critical mindset as a citizen-planner and ensuring that the endeavour is ultimately worth it (both as a process and in terms of outcomes wrought through the implementation of the Plan) is critical to success. Preparation and perseverance will be required to help keep the Plan on track and it is important to maintain momentum. This is to maintain interest and enthusiasm and to ensure that the evidence base, which underpins the policies remains up-to-date and relevant.

6.3 Managing expectations, resources and support

As we have stressed in Chapter 4, Neighbourhood Planning requires communities to maintain relationships with a number of local stakeholders such as local planners or developers, but just as important is ensuring that those orchestrating the Plan and the wider community are kept 'on board' throughout the process.

Support is the theme of this section and leadership is an important factor in developing and maintaining help – having a good command of the rules of the game is a key element here. A well organised and functioning Steering Group is instrumental in order to keep on top of the tasks as well as scanning for 'external' change that could impact on the project. We identify that good resources and support can lead to positive outcomes. Moreover, it is important to stress that Neighbourhood Planning is not like pointing a ship in the right direction and sitting back; many changes will emerge. Some amendment derives from the work as it evolves and some through the activity of others. This will more than likely lead to alterations of content, both in terms of the scope and in the wording, when compared to early aspirations or visions.

Research has consistently shown that in practice effective progress requires perseverance (particularly within the Steering Group), momentum and the visibility of progress (particularly for the wider community) and setting and adjusting realistic expectations (for everyone). For the Steering Group, this means being sensible about levels of capacity and commitment, the availability of key individuals over the course of preparing the Plan, and identifying and tying-down those whose skills are best suited to co-ordinating particular tasks. This resource-based challenge is accompanied by issues-based or substantive difficulties because the issues that are being addressed may not always be universally popular or some issues will need to be dropped or modified. It is likely that some involved in the project may not want to see this happen. In short the eventual Plan may not end up covering all the topics that the Steering Group or the wider community identify – partly because they may not all be within the scope of land-use planning or the evidence does not support it. This all underlines how Neighbourhood Planning is not immune to tensions and argument over what to do and how to do it.

Support within the community

Perhaps the most common challenge identified by Neighbourhood Planning groups to date has been lack of capacity within the Steering Group, with many Plans being prepared by a small number of people. Individuals often leave the group as they move away from the neighbourhood or life intervenes in some other way. In most cases such a situation is unavoidable, but try to prepare for this eventuality, for example, by ensuring that too much responsibility does not lie with one individual is vital to keep the Plan on track. It is also worth remembering that assembling a Plan can take a long time, often years (our research shows that a typical Plan will take just under three years to referendum if no significant delay is encountered), and so it is important to consider how each member of the Steering Group wants or is able to contribute over the long term once initial enthusiasm wanes or other challenges slow the process.

Internal skills

As discussed in the stages of Neighbourhood Planning (see Chapter 5, Section 3) the importance of project planning cannot be underestimated as it can help to make the process as manageable, efficient and effective as possible. The project plan can help groups to identify the specific tasks, indicate time-scales, skills required and stimulus to manage the relationship (and expectations) with other stakeholders involved in the process. It can help to ensure all involved have a realistic anticipation about the process, the commitment required and pragmatic expectations of each other.

As part of the project-planning process, it may be useful to conduct a 'skills audit' so that those with particular enthusiasm or skills pertaining to a task can be identified: this can be done in a very short space of time – and can be amended as the Plan progresses. Not all of the skills and knowledge required to produce a Neighbourhood Plan will be present within the community and a skills audit can help you to recognise the gaps. This can make the process easier and also help to identify specific 'one-off' tasks that the wider community may be able to assist with, for example, displaying posters or delivering questionnaires. This also helps to reduce the burden on Steering Group members. Indeed there may be 'expert' skills in the neighbourhood or linked to a community member that could also be prevailed upon, for example, a graphic designer to produce leaflets or a town planner who can assist with policy writing. This approach can then be used as a basis to draw in support from outside the community through, for example, the appointment of consultants.

Internal communication

Maintaining capacity and enthusiasm within the Steering Group is critical but a further consideration is maintaining support with the wider community. Ensuring that the community accompanies the Steering Group, as the work unfolds and issues are confronted, is important both in securing popular support at the referendum but also in making sure that consultation efforts yield representative results. Such general support helps to increase the chances of enlisting help when required by the Steering Group (or even co-opting others onto the group). Building and maintaining support in the community can be achieved in any number of ways, from chatting to neighbours in the pub to more orchestrated efforts, such as regular newsletters and developing a website. In larger neighbourhoods especially, it is important to ensure that the Plan is publicised as widely as possible and the use of social media (such as Facebook, Twitter and Instagram) can be a particularly cost-effective way of publicising the Plan and keeping the wider community informed about progress. However, this should not be at the expense of more traditional tools, for example, public meetings, leaflets and 'drop-in' sessions (as well as more innovative techniques and means; see Chapter 7). For further information and tips on how to engage with the community, including hard-to-reach groups (see Chapter 5, Section 3 as well as Chapter 4, Sections 2–3).

Community conflict

Dealing with objections or dissent can be a real challenge and due to the political and frequently conflictual nature of planning, even open and well prepared groups can find that support is fractured or not there when they need it. Dealing with issues such as housing or green spaces can be intensely political and it is unlikely that a citizen-planner can please all parties all of the time (even within small communities), and it is unrealistic to expect that the Neighbourhood Plan will reflect the views of all. However, it is beholden on Neighbourhood Planners to address the needs for the area, as actionable through land-use planning, and so evidence and local experience can really indicate the big issues. An important task is to inform all in the neighbourhood and enrol as much support as practicable. Meetings with groups or individuals to explain the issues can go a long way to build understanding and manage conflict. As discussed previously, openness and transparency in the process is essential in building and maintaining trust and avoiding conflict. Overall the community should be able to follow the Plan process and understand the decision-making process.

It is important to remember that the wider community may not know much about the intricacies of Neighbourhood Planning, or indeed the planning system more widely. There are a large number of resources that can be adapted and replicated and then used to develop support and understanding. It often proves useful to provide some straightforward information about what a Plan can and cannot do at meetings or online. Whilst even the most dedicated citizen-planner cannot expect everyone to speak to everyone or even learn everything about Neighbourhood Planning, being able to explain succinctly what a Plan is and what the Steering Group wants to achieve is an important skill that will prove highly useful.

Being realistic about what a Neighbourhood Plan can achieve for the community is advised: promising too much is destined to create disappointment later on and being overly conservative is unlikely to inspire much support. In this sense, Neighbourhood Planning is a tricky balancing act. This does not mean you should not be ambitious (see Chapter 7), but it is nonetheless necessary to be pragmatic so that the Steering Group itself does not expend energy and resources on pursuing policies that a Neighbourhood Plan cannot deliver.

In order to maintain support as far as possible within the wider community, the Steering Group should ensure transparency of process. This can help to maintain trust within the community and a clear audit trail should be maintained that explains the decision-making process (see Chapter 4). The Consultation Statement is equally important and provides the Steering Group with the opportunity to explain and demonstrate how engagement with the community and others has shaped the development of the Plan. This should enable the wider community and those with an interest in the Plan to understand the process that has been followed (see Chapter 5).

External support

It is not only support within the community that needs to be maintained. Key groups with an interest in and beyond the neighbourhood hold influence. The LPA has a key role to play in Neighbourhood Planning including a broad 'duty to support'. This means that they have a role to play in assisting, informing and ensuring that the stages are passed through in a timely and appropriate manner.

Evidence from communities to date has shown that support from Local Authorities is the key variable for communities in terms of the Neighbourhood Planning process. Local Authorities are undoubtedly best placed to support communities in terms of contextually relevant advice, however they also have wider responsibilities including strategic planning, development control and enforcement – not to mention a host of other local services. They have also been faced with cutbacks. This means that the support you receive from your Local Authority may not always be in the form you want it or at the right time. There have been some cases where the Local Authority is not forthcoming at all. This can occur for many reasons such as a lack of political will within the Local Authority, a lack of resources and capacity to assist, prioritisation of the Local Plan or even a community pursuing a policy or agenda that pits it against the Local Authority position. The relationship with the Local Planning Authority was discussed in detail in Chapter 4, including suggestions about how to develop a meaningful and clear relationship.

The first lesson here is that despite the vital role that Local Authorities can play in helping to produce a Neighbourhood Plan, they are not the only source of advice, support or capacity. There are a number of relationships that you may wish to develop in order to draw on expertise. The following tips, which make for the ENABLE mnemonic explained below, may assist in your endeavours to scope out the Neighbourhood Plan effectively:

- Early engagement: become knowledgeable about the Neighbourhood Planning process and the community – only when the Steering Group has a clear idea of what it is needed will others start to listen;
- Negotiate: the whole process is a form of negotiation, being aware of this and trying to understand what others are saying is vital for any citizen-planner;
- Ask: it is always worth canvassing for support from a range of sources – political influence and leverage for example can be important, so this might include talking to the local MP or Councillor(s);
- Branch out: speaking to other groups in the area can prove useful in avoiding missteps; and borrow ideas – for example, are other communities having similar issues, how have they been overcome and what positive moves would they advise?
- Lead: Neighbourhood Planning is citizen-led and the process cannot be pursued without the Steering Group's direction and pressure to ensure that progress is made;
- Enrol: support can also be brought in in the form of consultants – not only to provide capacity but also to advise on the process and explain the norms and intricacies of the planning system.

Other organisations exist that are able to provide support, notably Locality, the National Association of Local Councils (NALC), Action with Communities in Rural England (ACRE) and other voluntary groups (such as other Neighbourhood Planning groups both locally and nationally and various Neighbourhood Planning networks including the Neighbourhood Planning Champions), but also private-sector organisations like planning consultants. In fact there are many sources of support that can be drawn on and Steering Groups should not be shy about asking for advice and guidance (see also Chapter 9, Sections 5 and 6).

The number of Neighbourhood Plans that have successfully navigated the process is ever increasing – which means that there is a wealth of best practice, experience and knowledge built up within communities. It is likely that other groups have faced similar challenges or issues and you may wish to draw on their experiences. A steer and guidance can be sought from the templates, resources and material published by Locality and Planning Aid England (amongst others), guides and protocols published by other Local Planning Authorities, examiners' reports, 'made' Neighbourhood Plans and their supporting documents (including the Basic Conditions Statement and Consultation Statement). A critical mindset should be retained when reviewing this information and it is likely that it will have to be adapted to reflect your particular circumstances. There may be more than one approach that can be adopted, and if this is the case you may wish to discuss the options with the Local Planning Authority or consultant (if applicable) – you may find that this elicits a better response than asking the question 'what shall we do?'

It is also worth thinking outside the box when assessing possible sources of support – a good example is to approach a local university (especially if it has a planning department) to enquire what community support they offer. There are now plenty of examples of universities, particularly students, being involved with Neighbourhood Planning, ranging from embedded planning students within Steering Groups to providing technical aspects of the evidence base (see Chapter 9 for examples). We highlight two in Example 6.1, overleaf, which illustrates how students and university staff can help – both in town planning specifically and in related disciplines and knowledge areas.

Example 6.1   **Students and Neighbourhood Planning**

Local institutions such as universities are often willing to be involved. This will however be influenced by the time commitment, skills and expertise required and when input is needed. Both Oxford Brookes University and University College London (UCL) have assisted communities in the development of their Plans.

- Students at Oxford Brookes assisted Headington Neighbourhood Forum for over two years. Students helped the Forum's topic working groups to develop their preferred options for land-use policies and projects for consultation. Their ongoing involvement provided vital support and enthusiasm for the Plan and enabled students to gain invaluable experience.

- Students at UCL have worked in small groups and assisted a number of designated or embryonic Neighbourhood Forums in London. The support provided depended on the needs of the group and included assisting with mapping, carrying out surveys and digesting and explaining planning policy documents.

These examples are based on Planning Aid England case studies, see:
Oxford Brookes: www.ourneighbourhoodplanning.org.uk/case-studies/view/475
UCL: www.ourneighbourhoodplanning.org.uk/case-studies/view/486

Wherever external support can be identified, it is important to realise that a lack of Local Authority support, whilst unfortunate, is not the end of a Neighbourhood Plan. Indeed the original ethos of Neighbourhood Planning was based on communities 'taking control' of local planning rather than being overly dependent on local planning services. Numerous cases are available online that highlight this point (see Chapter 9, Section 5).

If the Steering Group finds itself in a situation of conflict due to seemingly intractable issues it may be worth considering mediation. This method of conflict resolution can take a number of forms, from informal face-to-face discussion with an independent party to more formal arrangements with professional mediation services. In all instances it always worth meeting in person, as meaning can be lost in other forms of communication and there is no substitute for face-to-face interaction. In areas with particularly contentious planning issues the use of such services is not uncommon and should be considered a positive step to help maintain the process rather than as a last resort. In such situations it is more important than ever that the Steering Group is aware of the wider community's wishes – in particular the positions that are strongly held and those that are less so.

During any process of conflict resolution the most important point to keep in mind is how to move things forward. Concurrently, the views and attitudes of local people will bring with it information or intelligence about what is important and what the priorities are for local people. Melding these inputs and keeping up progress is a skilful enterprise. In instances where the Steering Group has lost support from sections of the community or the Local Planning Authority – and has tried the methods above to maintain relationships and keep future options open – this should not mean the end of your Plan. While it is advisable to listen to the advice being given, the Steering Group can always take a different view. Where this is done make sure that you explain why you have not taken on board (some of) the advice. This can be recorded in the formal consultation statement, but do ensure transparency of process by recording and publicising key decisions as they are made. Ensure you provide adequate evidence to support your approach. The independent examiner can then act as the final arbiter at the examination stage.

—
6.4 Translating community aspirations

At its heart, Neighbourhood Planning is about integrating local knowledge into the formal planning system. Community-led planning is often accompanied by rather bombastic rhetoric about community control. Neighbourhood Planning does give communities some say over local planning issues, but it does not give communities or the Steering Groups carte blanche over local policy. Rather a degree of control is enabled by integrating ideas, desires and knowledge into the wider planning system. This can prove difficult for communities, especially at the beginning of the process and when it comes to putting pen to paper on planning policies.

That is why a cross-cutting theme of this book is integration. This has a number of meanings, but perhaps the most concrete example of this in practice is the integration of community aspirations into a language that is understood by professional planners and crucially that stands up to the rigours of the planning system. In part this refers to the way in which the development industry will often challenge and contest any ambiguities or gaps in policy to their advantage.

Many citizen-planners have a firm idea of what they want to achieve, and often after community consultation have even more ideas and a clearer mandate to pursue the community's wishes, but it can then feel very daunting to express these desires in ways that professional planners will accept. As highlighted in Chapter 5 when you begin to have a clear idea about what it is the community wants to achieve, it is always worth considering whether a Neighbourhood Plan is the right or only tool to suit the agenda. Neighbourhood Plans are not the only, nor necessarily the best, tool available for communities wishing to exercise control in the planning system, so do ensure that you have considered all options before you use up your resources and motivation (a list of alternatives is indicated in brief in the Glossary).

Should you decide on a Neighbourhood Plan, the process of translation from desires to formal planning language can be a frustrating one, but it is important to bear in mind that the more specific, clear and concise the Plan is – particularly when it comes to policies themselves – the more likely it is that you will achieve your aims. A concrete example of this challenge is encountered by many groups: a Steering Group may have orchestrated a successful consultation event and received a lot of useful feedback from the community – and is left with a collection of stick-it notes, survey responses, emails and memories of a variety of conversations. You may then reflect on a critical point: how is this information distilled into a planning policy? There are a number of general but important steps to take to ensure your data trail and the process followed is clear:

- Make a plan of action (as well as an overall Plan timetable), and have an idea about when and how much consultation you should undertake;
- Keep a detailed record of all the consultation exercises undertaken (especially formal events, surveys and the like) including how they were publicised;
- Keep all the consultation data well organised and backed up;
- Analyse the raw data so that themes and options for particular issues begin to emerge – record these issues in plain English. These can form the 'policy intent' and should be based on the following considerations:
    - What is the policy to achieve?
    - What needs to happen?
    - What does the policy need to do?
- Ensure the rationale is clear – the 'policy intent' can be included in the supporting text, which sits either above or below the policy, and will help the decision-maker to interpret the policy as intended and ensure the aspirations of the community are included in plain English;
- Connection or 'nexus' between the evidence and the policy – cross-check the policy intent with the evidence base and the existing planning policy framework. This will enable you to ascertain whether a policy could be supported (i.e. whether there is adequate evidence to substantiate the policy, whether it would be in accordance with the existing planning policy framework and whether it would add value);
- Begin to draft your planning policies (having a look at the wording in 'made' Neighbourhood Plans or ideally the Local Plan can assist here) – enlist Local Authority help at least once during this process;
- Provide feedback to the community – ensure draft policies are in keeping with the wider community's aspirations;
- Finesse and finalise the policies for the draft Plan – talk to a policy planner either in the Local Planning Authority or a volunteer from elsewhere – or indeed this is one area of activity where many Neighbourhood Planning groups have turned to consultants.

This list is understandably generalised and citizen-planners may find that they do not progress through it all chronologically or in a linear fashion. The process of producing policies is typically an iterative one that may include many revisions, alterations and draft policies (as indicated, these are often developed in conjunction with a consultant or with a local planning officer). There are two important lessons here: first, to keep detailed records of consultation activity as this will avoid much more difficult tasks later on; second, throughout this process there will be pressure from various stakeholders to prioritise their viewpoint (likely planning professionals and community groups but also potentially developers, landowners and others too). The Steering Group's job is to mediate between these competing interests and keep good communications going.

This can be a taxing and time-consuming exercise but ultimately it is the only way that your Plan will reflect the community's wishes and be workable as a statutory planning document. The reason that this process can be so challenging is the use of technical language that the wider planning system adopts. Many Neighbourhood Planning groups refer to this as 'planning speak' or 'planning jargon'; it can be dense and hard to understand but ultimately it is unavoidable.

Example 6.2   **Formulating planning policies**

Some neighbourhoods have found that the type of advice here would have been invaluable when it came to policy writing:

- West Hoathly, West Sussex – the development of the Neighbourhood Plan was an iterative process as the Steering Group sought to address the views and concerns of the community. Communication and openness about the direction of the Plan, emerging policies, evidence and robustness of process were essential to maintaining support and trust in the process;

- Birdham, West Sussex – sub-groups were formed and tasked with formulating planning policies to deliver the objectives. A volunteer 'writer' then pulled the document together to ensure the Plan gelled. That role was seen to be very important and necessary.

These examples are based on Planning Aid England case studies, see:
West Hoathly: www.ourneighbourhoodplanning.org.uk/case-studies/view/544
Birdham: www.ourneighbourhoodplanning.org.uk/case-studies/view/381

It is advisable to also look at a 'made' Plan that has been held up as an example of clear policy. For example, Tattenhall, Cheshire http://tattenhallpc.co.uk/wp-content/uploads/2013/07/Tattenhall-Neighbourhood-Plan.pdf. Please note however that Tattenhall Neighbourhood Plan was subsequently challenged by developers on account of the process followed (see Chapter 6, Section 4).

Throughout this process, critical citizen-planners should remember that it is their Plan, it is 'owned' and authored by the community, but it does not exist in isolation and it has to cohere with the wider planning system. A useful way to focus on this is to remember that once your Plan is completed and adopted ('made') by the LPA, it will be used by a local planner to make important decisions. This is most likely a person whom you have never met before and may not know your neighbourhood particularly well. You should therefore write with this future decision-maker in mind – how would a planner interpret this? Does the Plan's wording really mean what you think it does? For many groups, this process of policy writing and translation is the most likely stage to bring in outside help, either from Neighbourhood Planning groups that have already completed their Plan, local planning officers or from planning consultants. More detailed information on how to construct a planning policy was provided in Chapter 5.

Having gone through the process of developing the planning policies it is likely that there will be issues of importance to the community that cannot be addressed in the Neighbourhood Plan. This is often because they do not relate to land use or that deliverability over the Plan period cannot be demonstrated. If this situation arises consider including these as 'community aspirations' or 'community projects' in a separate section of the Neighbourhood Plan or as an appendix. These will not be assessed at examination and will not form part of the statutory

development plan document, however, they may form the
basis for future community action examples, which are discussed
in Chapter 7.

6.5 Technical challenges: making it a reality

Above we focused on taking evidence through to writing the
Plan, here we take a step back and consider the more technical
elements involved – particular tasks and studies that you will
need to progress through in the appropriate way. It is not the
intention here to provide a full manual as these challenges can
be diverse and area specific. What we wish to highlight is that
the greatest challenges most citizen-planners will face during
Neighbourhood Planning, or indeed most community-led
planning initiatives, will be technical in nature. However there is a
reason this chapter began with a discussion around maintaining
resources and support, and that is because knowing when a
neighbourhood requires additional assistance is vital to
overcoming technical issues. As we noted in the previous section,
the planning system can seem labyrinthine. Professional planners
can often appear to speak a language that only they can
understand, and this often manifests itself in specific planning
tasks and documents with which you may come into contact.

In many instances, Local Authority planners will be able to
assist you in understanding such technical components and
associated issues (as indeed could many consultants) or you may
be fortunate to have planning expertise within your community
that you can draw. Nonetheless it is important citizen-planners
have some understanding of these reports, what they mean and
how they interact and shape with the Plan and the approach to
take. To do this, you can refer to the relevant Resources sections
in Chapter 9 and the Glossary at the back of the book.

There is a warning implied here, however. Studying the
planning system often involves a steep learning curve and a
substantial amount of effort – yet it is not a citizen-planner's
duty, even when undertaking a Neighbourhood Plan, to become a
planning professional. Under Neighbourhood Planning, Steering
Group members' principal role is to articulate their aspirations

and do their part to 'co-produce' a Plan (there is more on co-production in Chapter 4). With this in mind, it is important to ensure that the Local Authority (also bearing in mind its duty to support communities) is not placing undue expectations on the Steering Group to 'professionalise' the work. This process, as with much else in relation to Neighbourhood Planning, is a balancing act that requires forethought and consideration.

Building the evidence base

There will be existing reports and sources of evidence that can be drawn on or if not available may need to be commissioned. These provide data that give a picture of the dynamics and needs – as well as opportunities – for the community. This is a wide category that covers many possible items and can include:

- Economic: e.g. business surveys, viability, vacancy/floorspace survey, available sites survey, land values, employment need survey;
- Social/Community: e.g. housing condition survey, housing needs survey, audit of community facilities, 'Building for Life' assessment of housing;
- Environmental: e.g. heritage audit, conservation area appraisals, review of local lists, urban design analysis, open space survey and analysis;
- Infrastructure: e.g. transport linkages, school capacities, transport capacity analysis, pedestrian flow surveys.

The above list is only indicative since specific policies will require specific evidence, however it is nonetheless important and needs to be carefully considered as evidence is crucial in Neighbourhood Planning.

As discussed in Chapter 5, Section 4, there are a number of sources of evidence that could be drawn on. To assist groups Planning Aid England has produced a useful diagram of 'sources of data and statistics', and see Chapter 9, Section 5. Advice that has been created to assist and clarify what evidence will be accepted by Neighbourhood Plan examiners indicates that opinion, or unsubstantiated assertion purporting to be evidential, is likely to be disregarded. Example 6.3 lists the items that are needed in relation to informing and supporting the policies and the draft Plan.

Example 6.3

Example Neighbourhood Planning documents

Bearing in mind our advice about future-proofing the work, an example list of planning documents or material needed to draw on or produce includes:

- Basic Conditions Statement;
- Consultation Statement;
- Local Plan (and the evidence that underpins it), plus national policy where applicable;
- Socio-economic data (such as the census, ONS data etc);
- Technical reports (such as retail and transport studies);
- Sustainability Appraisal;
- Strategic Environmental Assessment (where necessary);
- Environmental and landscape protection designations (e.g. SSSIs, AONBs);
- Design and Character Assessments or Appraisals (and see Glossary).

Developing options

Having reviewed the evidence and the results of community consultation it is likely that there will be more than one way of addressing the identified issues. For example, if traffic congestion has been identified as a concern this could be addressed by encouraging and supporting more employment locally or including policies to support home-working. Groups should try to keep an open mind as they go through this process as through discussion, engagement and thinking creatively more appropriate and innovative ways to address the issues and deliver on the objectives can be developed.

An area of particular contention and concern to groups is deciding on the most appropriate sites to allocate for development. As discussed in Chapter 4, Section 4, the starting point for many groups is to organise a 'call for sites', which provides an opportunity for those with land in their area to submit details of their land interest. Sites may also be identified from the Strategic Housing Land Availability Assessment (SHLAA) produced by the LPA.

A transparent and robust appraisal of these potential sites for development must be carried out. Clearly identified criteria should be used and applied to test each site in order to determine which is the most appropriate. The Local Planning Authority may be able to provide a list of criteria, and there are a number of guides and templates available that can be used as a framework, however, these will need to be modified to reflect specific local circumstances. This comprehensive site assessment process will enable groups to justify the site allocations. It is often the case that more than one approach or method can be adopted to test the options and therefore groups should also explain which method was adopted and why (see Example 6.4).

Example 6.4   **The Site assessment process**

Potential development sites must be assessed against a series of criteria to determine their appropriateness for development. It is insufficient to rely solely on the wishes of the community. There have been a number of different approaches to assessing sites including the following:

- West Hoathly Neighbourhood Planning group (West Sussex) formed a task group to focus specifically on the site selection process and appointed a consultant to assist: www.ourneighbourhoodplanning.org.uk/case-studies/view/544

- Ashurst (West Sussex) utilised a site assessment proforma (prepared by consultants) to assess the sites: www.ourneighbourhoodplanning.org.uk/case-studies/view/362

- Braughing Neighbourhood Planning group (Hertfordshire) appointed consultants to undertake an objective review of the site assessment process they had followed and their conclusions made to date: https://neighbourhoodplanning.org/case_study/site-assessment-support-braughing-hertforddshire/

Locality published Site Assessment for Neighbourhood Plans: A toolkit for Neighbourhood Planners, which provides further information: https://neighbourhoodplanning.org/toolkits-and-guidance/assess-allocate-sites-development/

6.6 Reflections

This chapter has highlighted the challenges inherent in community-led planning and Neighbourhood Planning specifically. Our intention is not to dissuade any neighbourhood from participating, but it is nonetheless important to consider the hurdles and roadblocks relayed in this chapter – overlooking these challenges can result in a prolonged process and more work for both citizen-planners (and Local Authority planners), with predictable effects on expenses, time and community motivation.

As we have sought to show throughout this book, Neighbourhood Planning is a balancing act, especially from the perspective of citizen-planners. At its heart this involves ensuring that the Plan reflects the views of the community as well as meeting the legislative requirements, including the Basic Conditions. Practitioners and academics often refer to these Plans as being 'co-produced', which in the most basic sense means that the Plan is a result of work from multiple parties, bringing their own skills and capacity, but also working together to secure a favourable result for all involved. This is why this book is themed around negotiation, integration and possibility, as it is these qualities that are central to co-production and making a Plan robust and worthwhile. It may be easy to consider such qualities as superficial or 'empty' but in practice they require forethought and dedication, as well as self-knowledge – by which we mean an ability to recognise both strengths and shortcomings in oneself or one's community.

In our research, many communities and Local Authorities (as well as other stakeholders such as landowners) have recognised the need for co-production in order to produce timely and robust Plans. However from the citizen-planner's perspective, the concept is not without its dangers. It is possible that – even with the best of intentions – community aspirations are lost as they become subsumed, manipulated or re-scripted into planning language. It is important to bear in mind that like all institutions, the planning system operates by means of a series of norms and expectations of behaviour (some more explicit that others), and in many respects the concept of community-led planning challenges those norms and the established way of doing things. Therefore whilst citizen-planners should be open in their communication and recognise co-production as a space of possibility, they cannot be naive and must at times assert the ethos of Neighbourhood Planning as community-led.

Embracing co-production can have concrete effects such as ensuring that the Plan and its supporting text is written in non-technical, accessible language that provides not only justification for the policy (i.e. in terms of evidence) but also a description of the community intentions for the policy. But it also has more intangible effects on the community's response to the challenges detailed above. Citizen-planners should be aware that they will, barring exceptional circumstances, require significant amounts of outside help – whether that be from other Neighbourhood Planning communities, organisations such as the Action with Communities in Rural England, private consultants or the Local Authority – but that ultimately maintaining community ownership may require proactive behaviours such as lobbying local councillors and ensuring that the Local Authority upholds its responsibilities. Becoming part of the planning system means recognising the roles and responsibilities of others (in particular local planning officers who frequently have high workloads and many pressing obligations and concerns) but also staking your claim to become an engaged part of that system.

Actions

In order to consolidate the coverage in this chapter, ensure:

- The existing evidence base (and possible gaps) is examined;
- That the development of a clear Neighbourhood Plan project plan is complete;
- Areas or issues of potential conflict are identified;
- What possible changes are anticipated during Neighbourhood Plan production (e.g. Local Plan reviews, reviews of national policy that are announced but not completed);
- That, if looking to emulate a policy idea, the policies as drafted are appropriate to context, backed by evidence and able to be implemented.

Chapter 7

**Opportunities and Ideas
for Neighbourhood Planning**

7.1 Introduction

This chapter concentrates on the third of our three themes: Neighbourhood Planning as a space of possibility. We highlight opportunities for innovation and to add value to the current planning system through Neighbourhood Planning, and recount ideas that citizen-planners can borrow, adapt and build on in their own Plan. Ultimately, adding value to the planning system through securing a community voice and shaping local development is what Neighbourhood Planning is about, and this Chapter will help explain what this can look like in practice.

7.2 Innovation and adding value

Empowering communities to produce a Neighbourhood Plan offers an opportunity for 'new ways of doing planning'. While a formal process has to be followed many groups are taking the opportunity to engage and consult with communities in more innovative and inclusive ways and to look at developing distinctive and progressive policies. Whilst Neighbourhood Plans must be integrated into the wider planning system (see Chapter 3), it is only by adding value and securing community aims that Plans become worthwhile.

Plans can be wide or narrow in scope, featuring a small or much larger number of policies and be more or less ambitious. To date, the number of policies in 'made' Neighbourhood Plans has ranged from 2 to 114 and their ambition has ranged from focusing on a single issue to much more extensive Plans. Useful examples include Wolverton Neighbourhood Plan and the CMK

Alliance Plan, both of which focus on Milton Keynes town centre, and 'mini-Local Plans' that include wide-ranging policies and which allocate areas of land for development, such as Winsford Neighbourhood Plan, Cheshire and Thame Neighbourhood Plan, Oxfordshire. The disparate nature of these Plans highlights how adding value to planning outcomes and the built environment may not necessarily be about the quantity or range of content in the Plan. How policies act in concert, or finessing a 'root' policy found in national or Local Plan policy can also provide value.

This brings us to a key point about the context in which a Neighbourhood Plan is developed: the presence of an up-to-date Local Plan or not. There continues to be an extended debate on the use of Neighbourhood Plans where a Local Plan is absent and there are several key things here for citizen-planners to consider:

- What is the timescale for the relevant Local Plan? (and how feasible is it to delay the Neighbourhood Plan, or synchronise with the Local Plan);
- Is there a willingness, if the Local Plan is absent, for the LPA to support the Neighbourhood Plan in its development?
- If the decision is to proceed, is there a willingness to review or refresh the Neighbourhood Plan when the relevant Local Plan is completed?

The short version of this debate is that a Neighbourhood Plan can be produced whatever the status of the Local Plan. However, it is important for citizen-planners to find out from the LPA what this status is, and how it might affect the Neighbourhood Plan. For example, an emerging Local Plan may be allocating additional housing to a particular neighbourhood or even allocating sites.

Beyond questions of calibration with the Local Plan, the conformity with national policy and legal precedence is also important – critical in fact. Even some of the examples we cite here may well be found wanting as policy and legal judgements act to reshape the space of Neighbourhood Plans. This is why we stressed in Chapter 1 the importance of realising the contingent nature of the policy landscape into which a Neighbourhood Plan might emerge. For better or worse, national and local policies can change right up to the moment a Neighbourhood Plan is made (and of course after!). Citizen-planners must be sensitive to this reality, resilient enough to persevere even if the situation changes and flexible enough to secure the community's aims in the best way possible.

When shaping the Plan, the geography and socio-economic status of the neighbourhood will also affect the issues to address. For instance, much of the Spring Boroughs area in Northampton features a post-war housing estate and the Neighbourhood Plan centres on a regeneration masterplan. In contrast, the rural Upper Eden area in Cumbria developed a Neighbourhood Plan through a partnership of seven Parish Councils which focuses on rural affordable housing – as the Plan area is one of the most sparsely populated in the country. The point here is that the value-added must come from the needs and characteristics of the area (and shown in evidence), not simply by attempting to adopt policies employed elsewhere.

Focusing on the issues of importance in the local area will also ensure the Neighbourhood Plan adds value to the existing planning policy framework and may enable a more 'radical' or 'innovative' approach to be adopted. By radical we mean the adoption of an approach that will address the specific issues in your area in a manner that may not have been considered at the wider Local Authority level (due to scale, and possibly resource allocation). It may also be that your network boasts knowledge and ideas that are not deployed by the LPA – this could be related to some innovations being inappropriate for the whole of a Local Authority area. To develop ideas, the use of visioning and techniques involving research and reflection are key.

Some Steering Groups are thus embracing the opportunity afforded to them to shape their neighbourhood. There is research that demonstrates a shift towards more innovative models of house-building through some Plans, as highlighted in Example 7.1, overleaf.

Example 7.1 **The impact of Neighbourhood Planning and Localism on housebuilding**

'...the emergence of new spatial practices in Neighbourhood Planning housing allocations...[the policy] gave licence to a model of house-building that promoted small-and medium-sized companies, affordable community-led and custom-build housing on previously developed sites. Neighbourhood Planning can be seen as a re-appropriation of space from the dominant market model with the neighbourhood emerging as the proponent of sustainability and social purpose in house-building.' (Bradley and Sparling, 2017)

Innovative approaches may be shaped around decisions not only about where development may go (i.e. through housing allocations, settlement boundaries or criteria-based policies) but also concern the type of development including the size of dwellings, tenure and occupancy. Some useful examples, which provide food for thought:

- St Ives Neighbourhood Plan (Cornwall) included a Policy on 'Full-time Principal Residence Housing' which sought to limit second homes and holiday homes;
- Tattenhall (Cheshire) Neighbourhood Plan sought to manage housing growth by allowing proposals of up to 30 homes (and no more) on sites – this policy was subsequently undermined as a result of a legal challenge (judicial review) centring on the process that had been followed.

Many Neighbourhood Plans include local connection policies to attempt to ensure that local need is addressed:

- Allendale (Northumberland) – where a local connections approach was cascaded so that the first priority would be for those from the parish, then from adjoining areas;
- Woodcote (Oxfordshire) – local connections were prioritised for the first 20% of affordable housing provided;
- Rode Neighbourhood Plan (Somerset) – includes a policy to enable downsizing through the provision of housing for the elderly within the community.

Such approaches to tackling questions of need will often be subject to increased scrutiny and therefore a robust evidence base and justification are ever more important. During the development of the Plan ongoing discussions should be held with the LPA and consultants (if applicable) in order to ensure the emerging policies accord with strategic policies of the Local Plan (or likely emerging policy), legislation and the NPPF – and overall meet the Basic Conditions as discussed throughout.

Indeed the issue of 'general conformity' with the policies in the adopted Local Plan has been a point of contention and was considered at the examination of the Upper Eden Neighbourhood Plan amongst others. The examiner's report in that instance emphasised the importance of the robust evidence base that should underpin policy (see Example 7.2).

Example 7.2   **Evidence to justify Neighbourhood Plan policies Upper Eden Neighbourhood Plan, Cumbria**

The examiner of this Plan concluded that 'the draft policy highlights a fundamental test of the extent to which policies in a Neighbourhood Plan can move away from national policy.' It also stretches the bounds of general conformity with current Eden District policy (where development of exception sites is restricted to those in sight of three existing dwellings rather than single plots), though not beyond what is reasonable. This decision was reached as the Plan is supported by a sound evidence base that promotes the thrust of the policy including 'the Housing Need surveys, the almost unanimous view of the priority to be given to affordable housing, especially for local people and the extreme nature of the Upper Eden with its sparseness of population.'

The skills in harmonising policies coming from within the community with those from above is a delicate but critical one. This is why we stress that crafting Plans that will be robust and compliant is a challenging aspect of Neighbourhood Planning, and in many areas some professional advice will be needed.

It should also be emphasised that Neighbourhood Plans do not have to focus solely on housing. Neighbourhood Planning provides the opportunity to think about the needs and future of the community in a holistic manner, with many communities

deciding not to allocate housing land. Research has shown
that around half of the Plans created in the first years of
Neighbourhood Planning had allocated sites for housing. Many
areas focused their attention on policies that seek to ensure
community benefits from future development. This may be
achieved, for example, by ensuring areas of importance are
protected (e.g. by designating areas of local green space), that
new development can be accommodated (e.g. infrastructure and
community facilities are in place) and the community is likely to
support the development (e.g. to ensure new development is in
keeping with the character of the area in terms of design and size
of sites). A Neighbourhood Plan may also include diagrams that
clearly explain the design principles that will be used to guide the
redevelopment of a site (see Figure 7.1). Communicating design
principles through words alone is possible but it can be more
effective when supported by a clear and engaging diagram
prepared over a map base.

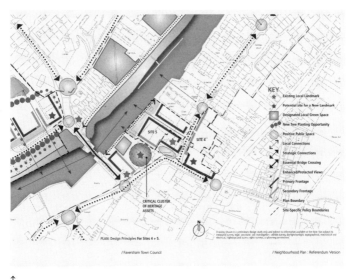

↑
Diagram to support planning
policies for the redevelopment of
sensitive waterfront areas, Faversham
Neighbourhood Plan, Kent.

Design and character assessments are often included as part of the evidence base and used as a basis to steer and shape development. These can aid local distinctiveness and a well prepared, positively expressed character study and associated policies should not be underestimated. An alternative to this is to work on a Village Design Statement (see Glossary), or collaboratively with the LPA to ensure a district wide Design Guide that can provide the necessary coverage. Many examples are available (see Chapter 9, Section 5).

Some groups are also taking the opportunity to build on the policies in the Neighbourhood Plan and to produce a Village or Parish Design Statement, which describes the distinctive qualities of the locality and provides design guidance to influence future development. In some areas this has been adopted by the LPA as a Supplementary Planning Document, which is a material consideration when planning applications are determined. This was the approach adopted by Nuthurst Parish Council in Horsham (see Example 7.3).

—

Example 7.3   **Building on policies in the Neighbourhood Plan
Nuthurst Parish Design Statement, West Sussex**

'During the preparation of the Neighbourhood Plan, research and surveys indicated that the vast majority of residents were keen to retain the unique and largely rural nature of the Parish. The Parish Council decided that the best way of achieving this was to produce a Parish Design Statement as an adjunct to the Neighbourhood Plan...Both the Neighbourhood Plan and the Parish Design Statement will be used by Horsham District Council to determine planning application.' (NPDS, 2017: p.4) The Parish Design Statement was subsequently adopted as a Supplementary Planning Document.

Innovation and creativity can also help inform a Neighbourhood Plan, as the techniques in Example 7.4 highlight.

—

Example 7.4   **Innovative ways of engaging with
the community**

Communication is key and different media offer help, for example, use of videos:

- To advertise the referendum, including 'Yes for Thame' (Oxfordshire) and Malmesbury (Wiltshire) Neighbourhood Plan Referendum;
- To explain the purpose of the Neighbourhood Plan (Lawrence Weston, Bristol);
- To explain the 'made' Neighbourhood Plan (Bude Stratton, Cornwall).

Music can also be a positive asset. A local resident in Spring Boroughs, Northamptonshire, wrote and performed a rap about the issues in the area and the importance of the Neighbourhood Plan. This was a novel way of raising the profile of the Plan, particularly in an area where traditional forms of engaging people, especially the youth, proves difficult. In Tattenhall, Cheshire, a music event was used to encourage participation, especially among the younger residents.

Mufti Games worked with Whitchurch and Hengrove Forum, Bristol, and built an 'engagement plane' as a mobile tool to aid the Regulation 14 (pre-submission) consultation. The key site to be allocated in the Neighbourhood Plan was a former airfield and the model aeroplane was used for an interactive consultation with passers-by and school classes. Use of the model plane had many purposes including drawing people in, allowing people to respond to planning proposals by writing on the plane, making it clear to residents that the Forum was leading on the Plan (not the LA), and to connect with a wider age range, including children. See: http://muftigames.com/play-in-housing-consultation/

The inherent flexibility in the structure of the Plan and topics that are identified also enables innovation in the 'framing' of the Plan. For example, the vision for Frome Neighbourhood Plan in Mendip District (Somerset) is to 'build a community that is resilient in its capacity to support the needs of residents in the face of global shocks such as economic downturns, rising energy prices and climate change.' Such efforts to tie into wider challenges facing society and are laudable. Good planning can play a significant role in addressing many social and environmental issues. Developing and harnessing evidence is all the more critical when and if innovative approaches are gestating and tying such policy aspirations to higher level policy is wise.

This brings us back to the idea of co-production and partnering with others who can assist in different ways. This is something that has been downplayed somewhat in published advice in the past. While the Plan should be 'community-led' this does not preclude identifying and enrolling the LPA or paid consultants for some element of the Plan, but more widely those people out there in the community who could help add value. A basic but informative example of co-production might be a charrette between local residents and professional planners where particular planning policies and ideas for innovation can be discussed. In such a situation, it may be that citizen-planners input ideas and community aspirations for the Plan and the professional planners discuss how these can be operationalised and expressed in planning terminology. Alternatively, the professional planners (for example, specialist Neighbourhood Planning consultants) might set out a range of planning policies and the community members might discuss their applicability to their neighbourhood.

This is a simplistic example but is indicative of the idea of co-production as we are using it here – where multiple parties bring contrasting knowledge, skills and ideas to the table with a view to achieving realistic and value-added planning policies (see other participatory techniques in Chapter 4). Using networking and tasking members of the Steering Group to seek out resources is another good way to proceed. Recall however that the essence of co-production, and of useful Neighbourhood Planning, is not to lose too much control to others.

——

7.3 Going beyond the Plan

While the ultimate goal may lie in achieving a 'made' Neighbourhood Plan, there are many wider benefits to preparing a Neighbourhood Plan. These include increased capacity, skills, confidence, contacts and knowledge within participating communities. These qualities – which can be grouped under the umbrella term 'community development' – provide a bedrock for future community action and should not be overlooked. Whilst we are wary not to encourage even more work for Steering Groups, it would be remiss not to capitalise on the ideas and networks that Neighbourhood Planning often forges. This has a practical side too, as producing a Plan often creates funding opportunities (and producing a Plan can be beneficial in bidding for funds from external sources) by raising the profile of your neighbourhood and increasing your visibility with the LPA, as identified in Example 7.5.

Example 7.5

Neighbourhood Forums as a platform for influence (Parker, Lynn and Wargent, 2017)

One unexpected thing is the notice that organisations have taken of us because we are the designated Forum – it gives us prestige and people take notice...[the developers] relationship changed when they knew we were designated – which went from 'irritated residents' association' to a 'proper player'. We had these linkages with the Local Authority and used those relationships and we could tell them we have support and so on. Formerly we [had] found out everything late.'

As well as building a profile for the community with the Local Authority, Neighbourhood Plans can also be a means of securing more immediate goals. While it is only land-use policies that form part of the statutory Plan, many groups include desired community projects (sometimes phrased as 'aspirations') in a separate section or as an appendix. These can form the basis of future proposals and work programmes once the Plan has been made. They can be used as a way to lever in CIL monies (where this policy tool has been taken up by the LPA) and to help lobby for provisions to be negotiated by the Local Planning Authority through a Section 106 planning agreement (see Glossary), and also as a basis to apply for funding from external organisations such as the Lottery or other charities and external bodies. Groups may wish to consider preparing an 'Infrastructure Delivery Plan' in support of the Plan which sets out the priorities for funding. The Steering Group also needs to ensure that they understand what CIL is and what the situation is within their Local Planning Authority – including what mechanisms are in place to access funding.

The inclusion of projects of aspiration speaks to our key theme of negotiation. Whilst Neighbourhood Planning projects are not legally binding on any party, their inclusion on a statutory document that has the backing of the community is a powerful tool in future negotiations with other stakeholders. Projects can also form the basis of new forms of local governance.

A number of Neighbourhood Planning groups have established a Community Trust or specifically a Community Land Trust (CLT) to ensure delivery of development proposals identified within the Plan. A CLT is a form of community-led housing vehicle that is set up and run by local people to develop and manage homes as well as other assets, whereas a Community Trust is a business entity established for the administration of funds placed in trust for public benefit. There is now a rich source of information on CLTs that can be investigated by any Neighbourhood Planning group who might like to pursue local asset management. Following the making of the Exeter St James Neighbourhood Plan (Devon), the Forum there set up a Community Trust in order to 'enable the projects identified [in the Plan]…to be turned from ideas into reality'. This approach led to the neighbourhood trust signing a lease with Exeter City Council for a garden as a Local Green Space. In similar fashion the Kirdford (West Sussex) and Broadwindsor (Dorset) groups set up a Community Land Trust to manage the delivery of their Neighbourhood Plans' objectives. In the case of Kirdford this was to ensure that elderly housing units and start-up workshops remained in community control. Whereas in Broadwindsor this mechanism was used to provide a small development of affordable housing for rent to people with a direct connection to the village.

Following the making of Upper Eden Neighbourhood Plan, the Kirkby Stephen Town Council took up another community right introduced under the Localism Act (2011) and produced a Neighbourhood Development Order (NDO; see Glossary) to expedite the development of a site. In this case the NDO serves to help implement policies and development proposals in the Neighbourhood Plan and allows for the reinstatement of a large residential building and the construction of off-grid dwellings for holiday letting or local occupancy.

This highlights the benefit of wider learning about the planning system, about issues and opportunities that are critical to making the best use of the Neighbourhood Planning tools.

Thus questions of health, ageing, the economic base of the area, and of socio-economic and demographic profiles are important examples of the understandings and evidence that will shape a Plan substantively. In process terms reflecting on these issues with questions such as 'what impacts are there for future development?' and 'what future investment is needed?' when brought together with the issues are useful as examples of the basis for good reflective plan-making, which can aid both the Local Planning Authority and developers in making their decisions.

7.4 Reflections

This Chapter has highlighted just some of the innovative potential of Neighbourhood Plans and the opportunity afforded to groups to develop locally distinctive policies that seek to address the issues in their area. Producing a Neighbourhood Plan can be a lengthy process and by focusing on the main issues of concern, time and resources can be put to the most effective use. Project planning and assembling as many resources as possible to aid the Plan is a key factor of success. As has been discussed, Neighbourhood Plans sit within a broader planning hierarchy and it is likely that many issues of concern to residents will be adequately addressed in national or local policies and hence do not need repeating in a Neighbourhood Plan. Conversely the limits that national policy and legal precedents place on Plans is that a difficult and possibly frustrating aspect can lead some groups towards a less innovative or progressive document.

It should be stressed that while there are opportunities and examples of policy innovation in Neighbourhood Planning to date, there is a need for authors of such policy to provide adequate justification and evidence to sustain innovation or new policy directions as they may be subject to increased scrutiny. Equally, persistence and the building of support is a counterpart to evidential tests. What we are stressing is that citizen-planners need to be aware of constraints as it makes the process easier in the long run. There is a tricky balancing act required to create a Plan that simultaneously adds value, is innovative and keeps the community on board – as well as conforming to the strategic policies from above and following the procedural and other regulatory rules.

Actions

In order to consolidate the coverage in this chapter, ensure:

- There is reflection on the way that other Plan areas have steered their Neighbourhood Plan and looked to add value;
- That the wealth of existing Neighbourhood Planning activity is used to stimulate thinking;
- That materials cited in the text overall and in the Resources area are checked back on;
- The networking and resource-seeking capacities in the Steering Group are developed; and
- There is reflection on some fundamental questions:
  - How do the community want the area to be in 50 years' time?
  - And *who* is it for?

Chapter 8

Reflecting on
Neighbourhood Planning

8.1 Reflecting on Neighbourhood Planning in practice

At the outset we established how Neighbourhood Planning features the three themes of *negotiation, integration* and *possibility*. Together these help indicate the mindset required to produce a Neighbourhood Plan successfully, and should be useful points for reflection for those wishing to pursue a wider project of citizen-planning. These threads are important and provide a shifting lens that highlights how each experience of Neighbourhood Planning will be unique – constraining as well as liberating those involved, as well as future beneficiaries. In this chapter we now draw together our thoughts and reflect on the process as a whole using these themes and linking these to the phases and resources involved.

It is worth reminding ourselves that state-led initiatives to facilitate public involvement in policy are always likely to exhibit limitations, not least government's desire to achieve its own goals. In this book we have aimed to provide a supportive commentary incorporating reflections on the role of Neighbourhood Planning within the wider planning system, the role of critical citizen-planners and some key lessons learned. Inevitably it can only serve as a starting point and a guide to what is a unique experience for each Neighbourhood Planning group.

8.2 The themes of negotiation, integration and possibility

Having explained what is involved in Neighbourhood Planning, the book's three themes can be interpreted and applied usefully. We have discussed how Neighbourhood Planning should be approached as a place for *negotiation*, *integration* and as a space for *possibility*. It is also important, in the spirit of wider community planning, that 'Neighbourhood Planning' is not simply equated with the formal, technical Neighbourhood Plan process. Hopefully this book has made clear that citizen-planners should first try and set aside any initial motives or reasons to mobilise the neighbourhood and to think about how the application of those themes can be applied usefully to their neighbourhood.

We have argued that Neighbourhood Planning is a *negotiative* process and should feature 'community-led negotiation' about the content and orientation of the Plan, as well as being acceptable as far as practicable to other stakeholders. Crucially, communities do not have to cave in to external voices when they are sure of their own views and motivations, and there are plenty of examples where Neighbourhood Plans have acted to reset the terms of engagement in their area through detailed or innovative policy. Ultimately, though, to realise such added value it is necessary for Plans to pass the Basic Conditions, in particular regarding evidence, conformity to strategic policy and exhibiting adequate consultation (tested at the examination) and community agreement (also expressed through the referendum). Think of these as quality criteria for your product.

Initial energy is important and we see that channelling some of this ensures that the potential and space of Neighbourhood Planning is explored and deployed as appropriate. Hence the theme of *possibility* – expressing ideas and options that seem good is positive; some may find their way into the formal Neighbourhood Plan and some may not and instead may stimulate other action. In short, a narrow focus at the beginning of the process to address a particular issue or issues can markedly affect how other matters are identified, voiced and then pursued.

This is why we have sought to stress the importance of *integration* (see right) as a key process in Neighbourhood Planning. As may be evident, we see processes of integration as closely linked with processes of negotiation. Entering into the process with an open mind is so important. Keeping a positive and inquisitive mindset throughout the process will allow citizen-planners to retain ownership of the Plan – but also crucially to maintain the enthusiasm and vision that will ultimately add value through the Plan. In this sense, the importance of a Plan can lie in its symbolic value for the community: as a tangible achievement that the community can be proud of, rally around and that will inform future decisions. Such a wider value may sound insubstantial and hard to keep in mind when dealing with the more burdensome and regulatory points in the process. It is critical though for both practical reasons (for instance as a bargaining chip or starting point in future negotiations with the LPA), and for creating and maintaining a local community identity, forging the ties that make local residents proud of where they live and stimulating participation in community life.

Where compromises are made these should always be in keeping with the prime considerations in view. This makes for a stronger Plan that will aid its implementation, as well as accurately express community aspirations and make it more likely to be seen as an achievement by the community.

8.3 Integration of views and policy

Despite being ostensibly community-led, citizen-planning is part of the wider planning system: hence our coverage in Chapters 2 and 3. As we explained, Neighbourhood Planning straddles two worlds: these can be thought of as the local and the strategic, bottom-up and top-down, or community and the state. It is Neighbourhood Planning's existence in and across these worlds that has led parts of the academic literature to talk about Neighbourhood Planning as being undertaken in a field of 'tensions' that pull key stakeholders – especially citizen-planners – in multiple directions simultaneously. Ultimately in practice these tensions require resolving, at least temporarily, and this means that Neighbourhood Plans need to be integrated into higher tier policy structures. As we have discussed, this can present difficulties for communities.

While the value of local knowledge is acknowledged and capitalised on, Neighbourhood Planning features a formal process that has to be followed with legislative requirements to be met. It is important that communities are not blindsided by jargon or cowed unnecessarily by expertise and hopefully, by reading this text, citizen-planners will already be inoculated against this. As discussed in Chapter 7, there is scope for innovation throughout the plan-making process, and within Plans themselves so long as it is evidenced and justified. It is acknowledged that Neighbourhood Planning may be constrained by the higher planning hierarchy but it also offers opportunity for groups to focus their time and energies on locally specific issues and to add value. They do not need to repeat policies in the Local Plan or general themes found in national policy given the Neighbourhood Plan forms part of the Local Plan.

At their best Neighbourhood Plans are formulated with governance partners working collaboratively to successfully reach the completion of a Plan. Thus a further point of integration is found on the philosophical level: Neighbourhood Planning is ultimately a product of the integration of different local and 'expert' knowledges in a form of co-production. As we have seen this involves sharing and integrating different knowledges and inputs and the resultant Neighbourhood Plan forms a hybrid as key issues, knowledge and expertise are negotiated. Steering Groups can become adept at applying evidence to the local context while keeping within the scope of the relevant Local Plan policies. In one sense it could be argued that there is no such thing as a 'local knowledge', at least not one unproblematic version of local knowledge. Rather the basis of the Plan is a (responsible) synthesis of various perspectives, understandings and views within the community, which also need to be deliberated upon and distilled into the Plan.

This reminds us of the call to maintain transparency and openness in the process and enable other voices to be heard. Steering Groups should not assume that voices of the Steering Group reflect the interests of all. It is essential that the Plan reflects the necessarily plural views of the whole community. In practice this can be a taxing and open-ended process of internal negotiation and integration, but it is also the fundamental strength of any Neighbourhood Plan: being rooted in a rigorous, transparent and open process of debates.

By the same token, knowledge and expertise mean more

than community wishes and views. Particular requirements of Neighbourhood Planning require a focus on land-use issues and that they be deliverable and implementable planning policies that are based on robust evidence. Equally Steering Groups need to be vigilant and ensure that they do not lose the aspirations and voice of the community whilst going through this process. We have offered tips on how to retain your voice and manage relations with others, both within and outside the community, as ideally the Plan has two outputs: first to be used in the determination of planning applications, and second situated within a broader vision and intentions for the future of the community as envisaged by the community.

8.4 Possibility (and innovation)

Neighbourhood Planning offers the opportunity for groups to shape their area, to produce locally distinctive policies that add value and address the wishes and concerns of the community as we indicated in Chapter 7. They also offer the opportunity to bring the community together with many benefits beyond the Plan. We have argued that despite the challenges that citizen-planners may face in terms of resources, support and energy Neighbourhood Planning is a real space of possibility. Perspectives that may be otherwise lost in the planning system can be brought in and put to use.

As we have intimated the product of negotiation need not be a capitulation; it has been demonstrated in numerous areas across England that Neighbourhood Planning can be used to deliver added-value, be the basis for further participation, offer up innovation, and provide a basis for challenge. Ultimately the realisation of an effective and worthwhile Plan will be the result of good research, discussion and deliberation. As such Plans can be:

- Sites of possibility to achieve the aims and aspirations of the community – including radical and innovative approaches beyond the Local Plan. Citizen-planners can grasp opportunities to add value, apply detail and focus on the key issues of importance;

- Sources for 'soft benefits' of participation, community cohesion and inclusion – which can broker resilience, be able to 'withstand' developer challenges and perhaps develop community identity (see Chapter 9, Sections 2 and 8) that make it more likely that the process is persevered with. This form of community development can help communities use further tools in the future, e.g. other forms of Community Led Planning, other Community Rights and to lever-in funds and opportunities to deliver on the Neighbourhood Plan;
- A store of community power where Neighbourhood Plans are used once 'made' – they are a basis for commenting on and influencing planning applications. Thus it is necessary to remember that planning law dictates that planning applications will be determined in accordance with the development plan unless material considerations indicate otherwise – this can easily lead to some policies not being interpreted exactly as intended.

It is important to keep in view that the planning context does not remain static – once the Plan is 'made' it is not the end of the process. In order for a Neighbourhood Plan to influence it will have to be maintained and this intimates a need and an ongoing process of monitoring, review and if required modifications. A 'made' Plan may act as a basis for further community action and participatory effort. Reflecting their place in the planning hierarchy, decisions affecting Neighbourhood Plans are made at higher tiers with the Local Plan in particular acting as a frame. It is therefore advised that groups use their gathered knowledge and expertise of the planning system to feed in and become involved in the Local Plan process. Furthermore, Neighbourhood Plans are influenced by broader changes to the planning system and it is advised that groups maintain a watching brief and remain informed by continuing to speak and work with the LPA, or by signing up to newsletters and bulletins published by others such as MHCLG or the support organisation Locality.

There are legislative processes and pitfalls involved in preparing a Neighbourhood Plan but also opportunities to effect the changes you want both within the 'made' Plan and beyond. Remember that, while there is a prescribed process, Neighbourhood Planning is not the process – the substance is the key.

8.5 Final thoughts

The purpose of this book was to highlight some key challenges of community-led planning, and more specifically Neighbourhood Planning, as well as providing potential solutions to those same hurdles. We hope to have prepared and encouraged citizen-planners to utilise the powers and opportunities on offer, but to do so in a more reflective and organised fashion. Figure 8.1 pulls together the key elements that we have synthesised across the chapters and shows how they inter-relate; that is the stages, or *phases*, are relevant in combination with the mindsets or themes – alongside the need to mobilise the variety of resources effectively.

The themes, resources and phases involved in Neighbourhood Planning

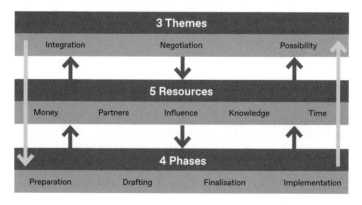

Figure 8.1 (Parker, Salter and Wargent NPIP)

Neighbourhood Planning, and the rules and parameters associated with it, is not perfect and there will be frustrations about bureaucracy, changing of goalposts, and so on. However, there are substantial benefits to engaging in the process, and the end product can be powerful. Many of these benefits are gains that are incidental; including the enjoyment of working with others in the community, gaining a better understanding of the place and actively shaping how the area will grow and develop in the longer term. If the themes, resources and phases are absorbed and then deployed effectively a strong Plan that reflects the priorities of the neighbourhood is much more likely.

If the decision to proceed with Neighbourhood Planning is taken, then having made it this far through the book and digested all the information here, we advise that revision and reflection on our initial questions is now undertaken:

- *What* is it that the community wants for the neighbourhood (and what tools are best suited to these aims)?
- What *resources* does it have at its disposal?
- What *skills* are needed at each stage? Are these within the community? If not, where can they be accessed? This may be within the community or externally (be that consultants, advice and guidance, tools and templates etc.)
- *How* can these be hooked into the plan-making?

Throughout this book we have drawn on our own experience of researching Neighbourhood Planning over the past eight years and also the extensive academic and practitioner literature available. These questions can act as a prompt for citizen planners to think beyond their neighbourhood with a view to the wider planning policy system and context – it is now up to them to decide what to do next.

Actions
In order to consolidate the coverage in this chapter:
- Look at the Resources section in Chapter 9;
- 'Plan to plan' – think carefully about how to proceed, not only what has to be done but *how* (consider an action plan to sit alongside the project plan);
- Develop strong relations with the LPA;
- Keep a note of what the issues are...and tell us about it!

Chapter 9   References, Resources
                       and Further Support

This chapter provides a list of useful resources organised by
theme for anyone interested in Neighbourhood Planning.
The resources are broken up into clear sections and markers are
provided throughout the text to guide the reader to the sections
that appear most applicable.

1. What is Neighbourhood Planning?
Explanation and critique (before you begin)

- The most comprehensive and up-to-date resource that
  provides an overview of Neighbourhood Planning is the
  Locality Roadmap *How to create a Neighbourhood Plan:
  Your step by step roadmap guide*. This was updated in 2018
  and can be accessed online:
  https://neighbourhoodplanning.org/toolkits-and-guidance/
  create-neighbourhood-plan-step-by-step-roadmap-guide
- Locality is a third-sector organisation that has been active
  in supporting Neighbourhood Planning since its inception.
  They are a delivery partner in the Government support
  contract and their website contains a wealth of information
  and resources on Neighbourhood Planning: https://
  neighbourhoodplanning.org/
- In 2016, the House of Commons Library published a
  detailed briefing paper including a useful overview of
  Neighbourhood Planning:
  http://researchbriefings.parliament.uk/ResearchBriefing/
  Summary/SN05838

2. Academic debate and critique (for a deeper exploration)

Neighbourhood Planning has been the focus of significant academic research and debate with different types of articles and papers published on many aspects of the process specifically, and the policy's wider significance. Most are aimed at a more academic audience (but often have a greater analytical content) and some are oriented to a practice audience.

- Crowd-sourced Neighbourhood Planning Bibliography: https://goo.gl/vkUzNC This is a more or less comprehensive listing of Neighbourhood Planning resources and academic references.

The following books or papers provide an overview and summary of Neighbourhood Planning experiences to date:

- Bradley, Q. and Sparling, W. (2017) 'The impact of neighbourhood planning and localism on house-building in England', *Housing Theory and Society*, 34(1): 106–118.
- Brownill, S. and Bradley, Q. (eds.) (2017) *Localism and Neighbourhood Planning: Power to the people?* Bristol, Policy Press. This book sets out a review and critique and features contributions from citizen-planners about their experience.
- Davoudi, S. and Madanipour, A. (eds.) (2015) *Reconsidering Localism*. Routledge, London. This book critiques and defines localism and discusses how it has come to shape urban planning. Leading academics contribute chapters and essay topics including localism and place-making, sustainability, social cohesion and citizen participation.
- Gallent, N. and Robinson, S. (2012) *Neighbourhood Planning: Communities, networks and governance*. Bristol, Policy Press. Draws on experiences of Parish Planning to examine the potential future of Neighbourhood Planning.
- Raco, M. and Savini, F. (eds.) (2018) *Planning and Knowledge: How New Forms of Technocracy are Shaping Contemporary Cities*. Bristol, Policy Press. This book explores the nature of knowledge required in planning, with

contributions showing how planning knowledge has become more diverse, cutting across public and private sectors, as well as citizens and communities.

- Wargent, M. and Parker, G. (2018) 'Reimagining neighbourhood governance: the future of neighbourhood planning in England', *Town Planning Review*, vol. 89(4): 379–402. This paper provides a useful overview of Neighbourhood Planning research between 2010 and 2018, and explores what a more ambitious form of Neighbourhood Planning might look like in the future.
- Wills, J. (2016) *Locating Localism: Statecraft, citizenship and democracy*. Bristol, Policy Press. This book explores the development of Localism as a new mode of statecraft and its implications for the practice of citizenship.

3. How/where is it situated and integrated? (before you begin and all the way through!)

The two policy papers that outline and explain the thinking behind Neighbourhood Planning are:

- Conservative Party (2009) *Control Shift: Returning Power to Local Communities*. London, Conservative Party.
- Conservative Party (2010) *Open Source Planning*, Policy Paper No. 14. London, Conservative Party.

The Planning policy and legal framework are contained in:

- National Planning Policy Framework (NPPF) (2018) www.gov.uk/government/publications/national-planning-policy-framework--2
- NPPF (2012): https://assets.publishing.service.gov.uk/government/uploads/system/uploads/attachment_data/file/6077/2116950.pdf (note: this will be superseded by the finalised NPPF 2018).
- National Planning Practice Guidance: www.gov.uk/topic/planning-development/planning-officer-guidance. Of particular interest and importance to citizen-planners are: Neighbourhood Planning, Local Plans, Strategic

Environmental Assessment and Sustainability Appraisal
and the Community Infrastructure Levy.

- Localism Act (2011) www.legislation.gov.uk/ukpga/
2011/20/contents/enacted
- Neighbourhood Planning Act (2017)
www.legislation.gov.uk/ukpga/2017/20/contents
- The regulations that shape Neighbourhood Planning are
likely to change and it is important to keep abreast of such
changes. In order to maintain knowledge the best way is to
regularly check www.legislation.gov.uk/
- MHCLG/DCLG (2015) *Plain English Guide to the
Planning System:* www.gov.uk/government/uploads/
system/uploads/attachment_data/file/391694/Plain_
English_guide_to_the_planning_system.pdf
- The Planning Portal contains a clear guide to the planning
system – www.planningportal.co.uk/info/200127/planning
- Planning Aid England – maintains an online knowledge base
with answers to common planning queries: https://planning
aid.zendesk.com/hc/en-us
- Locality published a *Community Infrastructure Levy,
Neighbourhood Planning Toolkit* that provides an overview
of CIL, the link to Neighbourhood Planning and a guide for
Neighbourhood Planners: https://neighbourhoodplanning.
org/toolkits-and-guidance/understanding-community-
infrastructure-levy-cil/
- Cullingworth, J., Nadin, V., Hart, T., Davoudi, S., Pendlebury,
J., Vigar, G., Webb, D. and Townshend, T. (2015) *Town and
Country Planning in the UK* (15th edition). London,
Routledge. This text sets out the basis of planning in the UK
and includes an account of its development over time. It is an
extremely useful reference text for anyone engaging with
planning. Always use the most up-to-date version – at the
time of writing this was the 15th edition.
- Parker, G. and Doak, J. (2012) *Key Concepts in Planning*.
London, Sage. This book is useful as it explains many of
the ideas and aims that permeate planning policy and
practice – and which are often contested and interpreted
in numerous ways.

4. Alternatives to Neighbourhood Planning

- Parker, G. (2012) 'Neighbourhood Planning: Precursors, Lessons and Prospects', *Journal of Environment Planning Law*, vol. 42 OP #139:20. This paper reviews the community-planning tools preceding and including Neighbourhood Planning and lists alternatives in a useful annex.
- RTPI (2011) *Neighbourhood Planning – existing tools*. RTPI, London: www.rtpi.org.uk/media/7334/Existing-Tools-for-Neighbourhood-Planning.pdf

5. Guidance and resources to assist in the process (particularly relevant to Chapter 5)

- Planning Aid England (PAE) and Royal Town Planning Institute (RTPI): www.ourneighbourhoodplanning.org.uk/
- A suite of '*Resources for Neighbourhood Planning: Putting the Pieces together*': www.ourneighbourhoodplanning.org.uk/resources/documents/29
- Locality: a large third-sector organisation that has been active in supporting Neighbourhood Planning via government funding: www.Locality.org.uk
- For an overall resource list see: *My community worksheets*: https://mycommunity.org.uk/wp-content/uploads/2016/08/My-Community-Roadmap-Worksheets-PR.pdf
- Neighbourhood Planning Independent Examiner Referral Service, Guidance to Service Users and examiners (2018): www.rics.org/Global/NPIERS_Guidance_to_Service_Users_and_Examiners_030418_hl.pdf. Provides an overview and explanation of the examination process as well as more detailed guidance and advice for examiners.
- Participation Compass lists consultation and participation techniques: http://participationcompass.org
- Historic England has drawn together a series of mini case studies on Neighbourhood Planning and the Historic Environment: https://historicengland.org.uk/advice planning/plan-making/improve-your-neighbourhood/neighbourhood-plan-case-studies/

- Insight about business-led neighbourhood plans is available at: www.ourneighbourhoodplanning.org.uk/case-studies/view/487
- It is not only the draft Neighbourhood Plan that has to be submitted to the LPA at the examination stage. Groups must also prepare a Basic Conditions Statement, Consultation Statement and the appropriate document to meet the requirements of the SEA Directive. Planning Aid England has produced guidance on 'How to write a Basic Conditions Statement' and 'How to write a consultation statement' as part of their suite of *Resources for Neighbourhood Planning: Putting the Pieces together*.
- Locality has published a guide to help groups, 'Understand if your Plan requires a Strategic Environmental Assessment': https://neighbourhoodplanning.org/toolkits-and-guidance/understand-plan-requires-strategic-environmental-assessment-sea/
- There are many Project Planning templates and examples available online including the 'PAS Neighbourhood Plan Project Management Tool' and Planning Aid England's 'Project planning template'.

6. Case studies and resources (particularly relevant to Chapter 5)

- MHCLG (formerly DCLG) Notes on Neighbourhood Planning – these are bulletins from the Neighbourhood Planning team within central government about latest news and policy developments: www.gov.uk/government/collections/notes-on-neighbourhood-planning
- Central government continues to provide funding to groups to assist them in the development of their Neighbourhood Plan. Details of the grant and technical support can be accessed here: https://neighbourhoodplanning.org/
- Locality is a third-sector organisation that has been active in supporting Neighbourhood Planning since its inception. They are a delivery partner in the Government support contract and their website contains a wealth of information

and resources on Neighbourhood Planning:
https://neighbourhoodplanning.org/. You can also sign
up to receive a quarterly newsletter on Neighbourhood
Planning.

- Forum for Neighbourhood Planning contains a wealth of
  information, detailed case studies, bi-monthly bulletins
  and video podcasts (to March 2018) to assist groups in the
  development of their Plan: www.ourneighbourhoodplanning.
  org.uk/
- Historic England provides examples where its work and remit
  touches Neighbourhood Planning: https://historicengland.
  org.uk/advice/planning/plan-making/improve-your-
  neighbourhood/neighbourhood-plan-case-studies/
- Neighbourhood Planning Champions a network of
  experienced citizen-planners who can give advice:
  https://neighbourhoodplanning.org/network/.

7. Relations with others
(particularly relevant to Chapters 4 and 6)

- The RTPI maintain an online Directory of Planning
  Consultants: www.rtpiconsultants.co.uk
- Dealing with consultants, advice from Planning Aid
  England 'Top Tips for appointing consultants':
  www.ourneighbourhoodplanning.org.uk/news/2013/10/29/
  Tips_for_appointing_consultants
- Commissioning Consultants – My Community:
  http://mycommunity.org.uk/wp-content/uploads/2016/09/
  Commissioning-consultants-final-version.pdf
- Dealing with developers – Planning Aid England – working
  with landowners and developers: www.ourneighbourhood
  planning.org.uk/storage/resources/documents/How_to_
  work_with_landowners_and_developers2.pdf
- The National Association of Local Councils (NALC) has
  published *The Good Councilor's guide to Neighbourhood
  Planning – designing the future of Local communities.*
- Examiners – NPIERS (a grouping organised to orchestrate
  Neighbourhood Planning examiners in 2013) produced a

guidance note in spring 2018 on this topic, with advice for communities as well as Neighbourhood Planning examiners: www.rics.org/Global/NPIERS_Guidance_to_Service_Users_and_Examiners_030418_hl.pdf

- Vigor, G., Gunn, S. and Brooks, E. (2017) 'Governing our neighbours: participation and conflict in Neighbourhood Planning', *Town Planning Review*, 88(5): 423–442. This paper explores the nature of participation in Neighbourhood Planning and concludes that one way to ensure a more open and free approach is to structure debate.
- Negotiation material can provide good lesson-drawing sources and we recommend the following books: Hoch, C. (1994) *What Planners Do: Power, Politics and Persuasion* (Chapter 7), American Planning Association; Fowler, A. (1990) *Negotiation: Skills and Strategies* (Chapter 1), Universities Press. There are now also some up-to-date and good resources online to aid teams working on complex projects.
- Locality has published 'Developing a Memorandum of Understanding: a toolkit for Neighbourhood Planners', see: https://mycommunity.org.uk/wp-content/uploads/NP_Memorandum-of-Understanding.pdf. Examples of Memorandums of Understanding include those published by East Riding of Yorkshire Council, see http://woodmanseyndp.co.uk/wp-content/uploads/2016/11/Memorandum-of-Understanding-Neighbourhood-Plans-November-2015.pdf, and South Somerset Council, see www.ourneighbourhood planning.org.uk/storage/resources/documents/East_Coker_MoU_final.pdf
- Examples of Terms of Reference for Steering Groups include those published by Rutland County Council, see www.rutland.gov.uk/_resources/assets/attachment/full/0/27124.pdf; Herefordshire County Council, see www.herefordshire.gov.uk/downloads/file/3719/guidance_note_28_setting_up_a_Steering_group; and Cornwall County Council, www.cornwall.gov.uk/media/15229978/Steering-group-sample-terms-of-reference.pdf

8. Experiences of Neighbourhood Planning to date

- Parker, G., Lynn, T. and Wargent, M. (2017) 'Contestation and conservatism in neighbourhood planning in England: reconciling agonism and collaboration?', *Planning Theory and Practice*, vol. 18(3): 446–465. Discusses how many Plans have been shaped and reshaped by the different actors involved – sometimes resulting in more limited Plans.
- Parker, G., Lynn, T. and Wargent, M. (2015) 'Sticking to the script? The co-production of Neighbourhood Planning in England', *Town Planning Review*, vol. 86(5): 519–536. An assessment of how citizen-planners experienced Neighbourhood Planning in the first three years of the policy.
- Parker, G., Lynn, T. and Wargent, M. (2014) *User Experience of Neighbourhood Planning*. DCLG/Locality, London. http://mycommunity.org.uk/wp-content/uploads/2016/08/User-experience.pdf. The first full evaluation of Neighbourhood Planning featuring the experiences of Neighbourhood Planning citizen-planners 2011–2014.
- Parker, G. and Salter, K. (2017) 'Taking stock of Neighbourhood Planning in England 2011–2016'. *Planning Practice and Research*. vol. 32(4): 478–490. Overview of where, and who, took up Neighbourhood Planning in the first five years.
- Parker, G., Salter, K. and Hickman, H. (2017) Briefing Note: *Neighbourhood Planning Examinations:* www.reading.ac.uk/web/files/NP-Examination-briefing-note-UoR-18-April-2017.pdf. Discussion of the role and issues with examiners.
- Parker, G., Salter, K. and Hickman, H. (2016) 'Caution: examinations in progress – the operation of Neighbourhood Plan examinations in England', *Town and Country Planning*, vol. 85(12): 516–522. Discussion of the experiences and operation of Neighbourhood Plan examinations.

Glossary

This glossary provides definitions and explanations of key concepts found in this text. Also included here are Alternative Planning Tools (denoted with asterisks) that might be pursued instead of or alongside Neighbourhood Plans. Entries are necessarily brief and so further reading may be required.

*Asset of Community Value (ACV) — local features, usually a building or land, that the community feel are important as the use of the building or land furthers social well-being or the social interests of the local community. They are nominated by the community for designation by the Local Planning Authority. Once designated the ACV is afforded additional protection and any development decision that directly impacts on an ACV must take this social value into account as a material consideration.

*Area Action Plans (AAP) — can be prepared by Local Planning Authorities to cover defined areas where particular needs or actions are deemed important. Some AAPs are prepared, for example where comprehensive regeneration is deemed necessary.

*'Article Four' directions — used to prevent changes of use that would otherwise be possible using the system of Permitted Development Rights (see below). An 'Article Four' means that specific controls can be put in place in a delimited area, typically for reasons of historic conservation but their use has widened.

Basic Conditions — these are the tests applied to Neighbourhood Plans at examination. They are discussed further in the main chapters, including Chapter 2.

Citizen-planners — our term used to denote members of the public who voluntarily devote time and energy to engage formally in the planning system. Notably by working on a Neighbourhood Plan. Such individuals can often assemble considerable understanding and useful perspectives about the planning process and community need.

*Community Governance Reviews — a process enabled after 2007 that aims to ensure that the best suited and most readily available empowerment opportunities and arrangements are reflected upon and in place to support citizens and community groups. This may include seeking to establish a parish in a non-Parished area.

*Community Infrastructure Levy (CIL) — a planning charge that can be used by Local Authorities in England and Wales to help deliver infrastructure to support the development of their area.

*Community Land Trust — this is a legal vehicle for owning and managing an asset for the benefit of a community. A wealth of experience has now been developed in setting such vehicles up.

*Community Right to Bid (CRtB) — introduced under the Localism Act (2011) this enables neighbourhoods and parish councils to nominate buildings or land for listing by the Local Authority as an Asset of Community Value (see above) and to seek to buy it under certain conditions.

*Community Right to Build Order — introduced under the Localism Act (2011) this allows neighbourhoods, if designated

Glossary

as Qualifying Bodies, to undertake small-scale, site-specific, community-led developments. This power gives communities the ability to develop such facilities without going through the normal planning application process.

Co-production — a concept highlighting where policy is developed in association with multiple parties and those involved, and their knowledge, being applied together to produce a strategy or plan. It intimates that each partner has a share of control and responsibility.

Delegated decisions — power devolved to Local Planning Authority planning officers to make decisions on behalf of the Council (i.e. without a planning committee deliberating on the case). Each Local Planning Authority will have a scheme of delegation explaining the categories of decisions that may be made under these delegated powers.

Department of Communities and Local Government (DCLG) — see Ministry of Housing, Communities and Local Government (MHCLG).

*Design Guide — not all planning authorities will have a design guide but they are often adopted as a Supplementary Planning Document (see below) and set out the more specific guidelines for developers regarding the features and preferences for building type, materials and other design features. This will most often feature illustrative examples of the requirements and add more detail than the Local Plan on design.

Environmental Impact Assessment (EIA) — seeks to protect the environment by ensuring that, for projects and development proposals that are likely to have significant effects on the environment, the Local Planning Authority has full knowledge of the likely significant effects and that these are taken into account in the decision-making process. A procedure has to be followed and this provides the basis to review, amend or mitigate a proposal.

Houses in Multiple Occupation (HMOs) — residential properties that have been sub-divided to accommodate more than one household, these may be rented properties where numerous rooms are let to tenants.

Housing Needs Assessment — this is the process followed to estimate the number of housing units required (needed) in a given area over a given time period. It is usual for this to be calculated in association with identifying a five-year land supply, i.e. the number of sites and units possible on each site will be highlighted in reference to reaching the housing needs figure which is 'objectively assessed' — see OAN.

Independent Examiner — this person will assess the Neighbourhood Plan against the Basic Conditions required to allow the Plan to proceed to referendum. The examiner is appointed by the Local Authority in agreement with the Qualifying Body.

Indices of Multiple Deprivation (IMD) — these are rankings of local areas, which are compiled and updated based on census data, to provide policy-makers with a relative indication of deprivation across all areas of the country.

Local Authority (LA) — when referred to here, the local government unit responsible for supporting Neighbourhood Planning (and producing a Local Plan). This is usually a District, Borough or Unitary Authority, i.e. the 'local council'. See also Local Planning Authority.

Local Plan/Development Plan — the assembly of planning policy at a district or unitary scale that includes the core strategy for the area. The Neighbourhood Plan when finalised will become part of the statutory development plan for the area. It is important that citizen-planners are aware of and input to Local Plans.

Local Planning Authority (LPA) — the Planning function within the local government unit responsible for supporting Neighbourhood Planning (and producing a Local Plan).

Material consideration — a planning term that denotes a factor that should be legitimately taken into account when making planning decisions.

Memorandum of Understanding (MoU) — an agreement drawn up by two or more organisations outlining the roles and responsibilities to each other and/or to a mutual project.

Ministry of Housing, Communities and Local Government (MHCLG) — the central government department in the UK that leads on planning and specifically Neighbourhood Planning (formerly known as the Department of Communities and Local Government or DCLG).

National Planning Policy Framework (NPPF) — the policy document that sets out the Government's main planning policies for England and how they are expected to be applied. Local Plans and Neighbourhood Plans must conform to the orientation of the NPPF. It was first produced in 2012 with a second version in 2018.

National Planning Practice Guidance (NPPG) — adds further context to the National Planning Policy Framework and informs all involved about the policy position relating to any and all relevant planning matters. It was formed in 2014 and is accessed online.

*Neighbourhood Development Order (NDO) — introduced under the Localism Act (2011) this enables neighbourhoods to identify sites or buildings to be granted planning permission for specified development in the neighbourhood area. Such Orders may facilitate community-inspired projects to come to fruition.

Neighbourhood Development Plan (NDP) — a plan produced under the provisions of the Localism Act 2011 and associated regulations in England. Such a Plan will be led by the community that it serves and meet a series of legislative requirements and Basic Conditions including conformity with higher level policy. We refer to these here as a Neighbourhood Plan.

Neighbourhood Forum — the body that leads on the production of a Neighbourhood Plan in neighbourhood areas that are not covered (in part or in whole) by a town or parish council. A Neighbourhood Forum must meet certain legal requirements and must be designated by the Local Planning Authority.

Objectively Assessed (Housing) Need (OAN) — Local Planning Authorities make objective assessments of the need for market and affordable housing in their area. The Local Plan should provide sufficient land to meet the OAN in full, insofar as it has the sustainable capacity to do so. The

OAN and housing target in the Local Plan serves as a basis for the 'five-year land supply' for housing purposes. A proportion of that figure may need to be accommodated within a Neighbourhood Plan area.

Permitted Development Rights (PDRs) — a system whereby developers can change use of an existing building without the need to gain planning permission. For example shifting from office to residential use or from agricultural use to residential. Numerous changes to this tool have been introduced since 2013 and qualifying criteria apply. Exceptions may be made through applying an 'Article Four' direction (see above).

Planning Aid England (PAE) — an organisation run by the RTPI featuring a mix of staff and planning volunteers, which provides advice to individuals and community groups involved in the planning system.

Planning Inspectorate (PINS) — an executive agency of MHCLG that deals with planning appeals, national infrastructure planning applications, examinations of Local Plans and other planning-related and specialist casework in England and Wales.

Qualifying Body — the formal body responsible for the Neighbourhood Plan. In Parished areas this will be the Parish or Town Council, while in non-Parished areas a Neighbourhood Forum will be constituted to undertake the Neighbourhood Plan.

Referendum (Neighbourhood) — as part of the Neighbourhood Planning regulations Neighbourhood Development Plans must undergo a referendum. This occurs after the examination and where the neighbourhood population vote whether to adopt the Plan not. If more than 50% of the community votes 'yes' the NDP must be adopted ('made') by the Local Planning Authority.

Royal Town Planning Institute (RTPI) — the professional body for town planners. The Institute, through Planning Aid England, has produced a lot of support information for Neighbourhood Planning.

Section 106 planning agreement – named after the relevant section of the (1990 Act)

enabling legislation, these are agreements made between Local Authorities and developers and can be attached to a planning permission to 'make acceptable development that would otherwise be unacceptable in planning terms'. In practice these act to secure certain benefits and undertakings to ensure public policy objectives are addressed through new development. It can be a means to secure community benefits.

Statement of Community Involvement (SCI) – the document that all Local Planning Authorities must produce, setting out their approach to community involvement. From summer 2018 the SCI must specify how the Local Authority will support Neighbourhood Planning groups in terms of the advice and assistance offered.

Steering Group – a small committee of community members that often oversees the Neighbourhood Plan on behalf of the usually larger Neighbourhood Forum or Parish or Town Council.

Strategic Environmental Assessment (SEA) – a means of informing and shaping the decision support process, to ensure that environmental and possibly other sustainability aspects are considered effectively in policy-, plan- and programme-making. This is a staged approach that aids modification of plans and policies. In certain circumstances it is a requirement for SEA to be applied in the development of a Neighbourhood Plan.

*Supplementary Planning Document (SPD) – a document produced to build on and provide more detailed advice or guidance on the policies in the Local Plan. Once adopted, it forms part of the development plan.

Sustainability Appraisal (SA) – a process of assessing options and policy drafts in the preparation of a Local Plan and a Neighbourhood Plan.

Sustainable Development – a key idea that underpins much planning activity in the UK (and beyond). Variously defined it essentially acts to signify that new development should not 'compromise future generations' ability to live and enjoy planet earth'. The purpose of the planning system is to contribute to the achievement of sustainable development and its characteristics relate to processes of policy- and decision-making as well as outcomes.

Use Classes Order (UCO) – this sets out the types of land and building uses recognised in the planning system. It is occasionally amended but covers uses such as residential, retail, industrial, and so on. Planning permission is usually required to change from one use to another although there are exceptions.

*Village Design Statement (VDS) – a tool largely for rural settlements to indicate their design preferences. Some Local Planning Authorities adopted such statements to act as local design guides, material considerations in planning applications or Supplementary Planning Documents.

Written Ministerial Statement – on occasion the Government will make announcements that affect some aspect of planning policy. The formal medium for those are the Ministerial Statements that are published to seek to clarify or adjust a policy issue.